Birth to 6 Months
Rattle Time, Face to Face, and Many Other Activities for Infants

Creative Resources Infant and Toddler Series

Dedication

THIS BOOK IS DEDICATED TO:

My grandchildren, Jeffrey and Eva Herr.
J. H.

My son, Randy, and my nieces and nephews.
T. S.

Birth to 6 Months
Rattle Time, Face to Face, and Many Other Activities for Infants

Creative Resources Infant and Toddler Series

by

Judy Herr Terri Swim

PHYSICAL

COGNITIVE

EMOTIONAL

LANGUAGE & COMMUNICATION

SOCIAL

THOMSON

DELMAR LEARNING

Australia Canada Mexico Singapore Spain United Kingdom United States

THOMSON

DELMAR LEARNING

Rattle Time, Face to Face, and Many Other Activities for Infants: Birth to 6 Months
Judy Herr and Terry Swim

Business Unit Executive Director:
Susan L. Simpfenderfer

Executive Production Manager:
Wendy A. Troeger

Executive Marketing Manager:
Donna J. Lewis

Acquisitions Editor:
Erin O'Connor

Production Editor:
Joy Kocsis

Channel Manager:
Nigar Hale

Editorial Assistant:
Ivy Ip

Technology Project Manager:
Joseph Saba

Cover Design:
Joseph Villanova

Composition:
Stratford Publishing Services, Inc.

For permission to use material from this text or product, contact us by
Tel   (800) 730-2214
Fax   (800) 730-2215
www.thomsonrights.com

Library of Congress Cataloging-in-Publication Data

Herr, Judy.
    Rattle time, face to face, and many other activities for infants: birth to 6 months / by Judy Herr, Terri Swim.
        p. cm.--(Creative resources infant and toddler series)
    Includes bibliographical references.
    ISBN 1-40181-832-3
    1. Infants--Development. 2. Child development. 3. Early childhood education--Activity programs. 4. Creative activities and seat work. I. Swim, Terri. II. Title. III. Series.

    HQ774 .H4756 2003
    305.232--dc21

                                                        2002031236

NOTICE TO THE READER

Contents

References   95

Appendices   96

Preface

Responding in a warm, loving, and responsive manner to a crying infant or playing patty-cake with a young toddler both exemplify ways that caregivers and families promote healthy brain development. In fact, recent research on brain development emphasizes the importance of the environment and relationships during the child's first three years of life (Shore, 1997). With this in mind, *Rattle Time, Face to Face, and Many Other Activities for Infants: Birth to 6 Months* was written for you, the caregivers and families. The ultimate goal of this book is to assist in promoting healthy development of our youngest children. Thus, it should be part of all parents' and caregivers' libraries.

The book focuses on the growth of the whole child by including norms for physical, language and communication, cognitive, social, and emotional development. To support, enhance, and promote the child's development in all of these areas, this unique book includes specially designed activities for infants. Note that the book has several sections. The first section includes information for understanding, assessing, and promoting development, as well as suggestions for interacting with young children. The next sections include innovative activities to promote development for infants. The last section includes references for the material cited in the text. The appendices are a rich resource including, but not limited to, lists of recipes, songs, finger plays, chants, and books. They also contain a list of toys and equipment, as well as criteria for making selections.

To assist you, the experiences are grouped by age ranges and developmental areas. Each of these activities is designed to illustrate the connection between a broad area of development and specific goals for children. For example, physical development may be the primary area and eye-hand coordination may be one specific goal. The materials, preparation, and nurturing strategies for the activities are designed for easy and effective implementation. Moreover, variations and additional information have been incorporated to enrich the experience for both you and the child. Highlighting Development boxes provide valuable information for fostering an understanding of young children's development. Collectively, the information and experiences provided in this book will enhance your ability to meet the developmental needs of infants, fostering optimal development of the whole child. Furthermore, these early experiences will create a strong foundation for children's subsequent thinking, interacting with others, and learning.

ONLINE RESOURCES™

The Online Resources™ to accompany *Rattle Time, Face to Face, and Many Other Activities for Infants: Birth to 6 Months* is your link to early childhood education on the Internet. The Online Resources™ contains many features to help focus your understanding of the learning and teaching process.

- Sample Activities and Preface
- Developmental Milestones
- Books for Infants
- Criteria for Selecting Materials and Equipment for Children
- Materials and Equipment for Promoting Optimal Development
- Favorite Finger Plays, Nursery Rhymes, and Chants
- Songs
- Rhythm Instruments
- Resources Related to Infants
- Developmental Checklist
- Anecdotal Record
- Panel Documentation
- Lesson Plan
- Daily Communications
- A Summarized list of Web links is provided for your reference.
- On-line Early Education Survey – This survey gives you the opportunity to let us know what features you want to see improved on the Online Resources™.

The authors and Delmar Learning make every effort to ensure that all Internet resources are accurate at the time of printing. However, due to the fluid, time-sensitive nature of the Internet, we cannot guarantee that all URLs and Web site addresses will remain current for the duration of this edition.

 You can find the Online Resources™ at www.earlychilded.delmar.com

ACKNOWLEDGMENTS

We would like to thank many people. First, our husbands, Dr. James Herr and James Daniel Swim, who supported us during this process.

To our families, who have continuously provided encouragement and facilitated our personal and professional development.

Furthermore, this book would not have been possible without the inspiration of the numerous young children who have touched and influenced our lives in so many meaningful ways. The children we have met in university laboratories and child care settings and their teachers and parents have all demonstrated the importance of the early years of life.

We want to acknowledge the contributions of the numerous colleges, universities, colleagues, and students that have fostered our professional growth and development:

College of William and Mary, Norfolk, Virginia; University of Akron, Ohio; Harvard University, Cambridge, Massachusetts; Purdue University, West Lafayette, Indiana; University of Minnesota, Minneapolis, Minnesota; University of Missouri, Columbia, Missouri; University of Texas, Austin, Texas; and University of Wisconsin-Stout, Menomonie, Wisconsin.

Specifically we would like to thank Carla Ahman, Carol Armga, Michelle Batchelder, Chalandra Bryant, Mary Jane Burson-Polston, Bill Carver, Linda Conner, Kay Cutler, Sandi Dillon, Loraine Dunn, Nancy File, Nancy Hazen-Swann, Debra Hughes, Susan Jacquet, Elizabeth Johnson, Joan Jurich, Susan Kontos, Gary Ladd, Julia Lorenz, Pat Morris, Linda Norton-Smith, Barbara O'Donnel, Diana Peyton, Douglas R. Powell, Kathy Pruesse, Julie Rand, Karin Samii, Jen Shields, Cathy Surra, Adriana Umana, Chris Upchurch, Lisa West, and Rhonda Whitman for their encouragement and support.

Also, special thanks to Carol Hagness, University of Wisconsin-Stout Educational Materials Collection Librarian, and Ann Salt, Children's Librarian at the Menomonie Public Library, who developed the list of books for infants that is located in Appendix A; Erin O'Connor, our editor from Delmar Learning who provided continuous encouragement, support, and creative ideas; and Deb Hass and Vicki Weber, who typed the manuscript.

The authors and publisher would like to thank the following reviewers for their constructive suggestions and recommendations:

Davia Allen
Western Carolina University
Cullowhee, NC

Alice Beyrent
Hesser College
Manchester, NH

Billie Coffman
Pennsylvania College of Technology
Williamsport, PA

Irene Cook
Taft College Children's Center
Taft, CA

Linda Estes
St. Charles County Community College
St. Peters, MO

Jody Martin
Children's World Learning Centers
Golden, CO

Introduction

Smiling, crying, bicycling with their legs, and laughing at caregivers are all signals infants use to gain and maintain attention. Watching them is exciting. They are amazing. Each infant has an individual style; no two are alike. Differences in temperament are apparent from birth. Some infants are quiet, while others are active. Each is unique. However, all infants grow and develop in predictable patterns, even though the exact rate varies from infant to infant.

Development can be defined as change over time. According to Bentzen (2001), development refers to any "change in the structure, thought, or behavior of an individual that comes from biological and environmental influences" (p. 15). Human development occurs in two distinct patterns. First, development proceeds from the top of the body to the bottom. For example, control of the head develops before control of the torso or the legs. The second pattern is for development to proceed from the center of the body outward. To illustrate, the arm muscles develop before those of the hands or fingers.

UNDERSTANDING THEORIES OF DEVELOPMENT

Searching the literature, you will find numerous beliefs about or theories of child growth and development. Some beliefs are in direct opposition to each other. There are theories that state children are biologically programmed at birth. These theories purport that children develop according to their own individual timetable, regardless of environmental influences. In contrast, there are nurture-based theories that emphasize the importance of environmental factors. These theories assume that children enter the world as blank slates. According to these theories, the children's environment is instrumental in molding their abilities. A third set of theories incorporates aspects from both of these two extremes, nature and nurture. These interactional theories are based on the premise that biology and environment work in concert to account for children's development.

While reading this book, you will note that it celebrates interactional theories. Current research on brain development supports the belief that human development hinges on the dynamic interplay between nature and nurture (Shore, 1997). At birth, the development of the child's brain is unfinished. Through early experiences, the brain matures and connections are made for wiring its various parts. Repeated experiences result in the wiring becoming permanent, thereby creating the foundation for the brain's organization and functioning throughout life.

Your role is critical because early experiences significantly affect how each child's brain is wired. The child's relationships with parents, caregivers, and significant others will all influence how the brain becomes wired. Therefore, loving encounters and positive social, emotional, language and communication, cognitive, and physical experiences all influence the development of a healthy brain.

However, this influence is far from unidirectional. Children, for example, are born with different temperaments. Research has shown that children's dispositions influence their involvement with both people and materials in their environment. To illustrate, Quincy is a quiet, slow-to-warm-up child. He initially holds back and observes. Moreover, he becomes very distressed in new situations. To prevent Quincy from feeling distressed, his caregivers and parents sometimes respond by minimizing the introduction of new experiences or situations. Consequently, his physical, language and communication, emotional, social, and cognitive development are shaped by his characteristics and his caregivers' and parents' responses to these characteristics.

USING DEVELOPMENTAL NORMS

Research on human development provides evidence that infants and toddlers grow and develop in predictable sequences or patterns. Such predictable, or universal, patterns of development occur in all domains—physical, cognitive, language and communication, social, and emotional. The specific components of these universal patterns are called developmental norms. Norms provide evidence of when a large group of children, on average, accomplishes a given task. Because norms are averages, they must be interpreted with caution. There are differences from child to child in the timing for reaching developmental milestones within one specific domain and across different domains. For example, a child may reach all developmental milestones as expected in the cognitive domain but develop on a later timetable in the language domain. Hence, each child has a unique pattern of timing of growth and development that must be taken into account.

Notwithstanding their limitations, developmental norms are useful to caregivers and parents for three main reasons. First, they allow for judgments and evaluations of the relative normalcy of a child's developmental progression. If a child is lagging behind in one developmental task, generally there should be little concern. But if a child is behind on numerous tasks, human development specialists should be consulted for further evaluations.

Second, developmental norms are useful in making broad generalizations about the timing of particular skills and behaviors. Understanding the child's current level of development in relation to the norms allows predictions about upcoming tasks. For example, a child who can easily find a toy that is partially hidden is ready to begin searching for a toy that is completely out of view.

This knowledge of future development ties into the third reason why developmental norms are helpful. Developmental norms allow caregivers and parents to create and implement experiences that support and enhance the child's current level of development. Following the example just given, an adult playing a hide-and-seek game could begin by partially hiding a toy with a towel and then add the challenge of completely covering the toy.

The following table includes a list of developmental norms for infants and toddlers, highlighting significant tasks. Norms are grouped by areas of development, and within each area the specific tasks have been arranged sequentially. When using this table, please remember that it represents universal patterns of development. You will need to be cognizant of each child's unique patterns.

Developmental Milestones*

Birth to Three Months	Four to Six Months	Seven to Nine Months	Ten to Twelve Months	Thirteen to Eighteen Months	Nineteen to Twenty-Four Months	Twenty-Five to Thirty-Six Months
Acts reflexively—sucking, stepping, rooting	Holds cube in hand	Sits independently	Supports entire body weight on legs	Builds tower of two cubes	Walks up stairs independently, one step at a time	Maneuvers around obstacles in a pathway
Swipes at objects in front of body, uncoordinated	Reaches for objects with one hand	Stepping reflex returns, so that child bounces when held on a surface in a standing position	Walks when hands are held	Turns the pages of a cardboard book two or three at a time	Jumps in place	Runs in a more adult-like fashion; knees are slightly bent, arms move in the opposite direction
Holds head erect and steady when lying on stomach	Rolls from back to side	Leans over and reaches when in a sitting position	Cruises along furniture or steady objects	Scribbles vigorously	Kicks a ball	Walks down stairs independently
Lifts head and shoulders	Reaches for objects in front of body, coordinated	Gets on hands and knees but may fall forward	Stands independently	Walks proficiently	Runs in a modified fashion	Marches to music
Rolls from side to back	Sits with support	Crawls	Walks independently	Walks while carrying or pulling a toy	Shows a decided preference for one hand	Uses feet to propel wheeled riding toys
Follow moving objects with eyes	Transfers objects from hand to hand	Pulls to standing position	Crawls up stairs or steps	Walks up stairs with assistance	Completes a three-piece puzzle with knobs	Rides a tricycle
	Grabs objects with either hand	Claps hands together	Voluntarily releases objects held in hands		Builds a tower of six cubes	Usually uses whole arm movements to paint or color
	Sits in tripod position using arms for support	Stands with adult's assistance	Has good balance when sitting; can shift positions without falling			Throws ball forward, where intended
		Learns pincer grasp, using thumb with forefinger to pick up objects	Takes off shoes and socks			Builds tower using eight or more blocks
		Uses finger and thumb to pick up objects				Imitates drawing circles and vertical and horizontal lines
		Brings objects together with banging noises				Turns pages in book one by one
						Fingers work together to scoop up small objects
						Strings large beads on a shoelace

*The developmental milestones listed are based on universal patterns of when various traits emerge. Because each child is unique certain traits may develop at an earlier or later age.

Developmental Milestones * (continued)

LANGUAGE AND COMMUNICATION DEVELOPMENT

Birth to Three Months	Four to Six Months	Seven to Nine Months	Ten to Twelve Months	Thirteen to Eighteen Months	Nineteen to Twenty-Four Months	Twenty-Five to Thirty-Six Months
Communicates with cries, grunts, and facial expressions	Babbles spontaneously	Varies babble in loudness, pitch, and rhythm	Uses preverbal gestures to influence the behavior of others	Has expressive vocabulary of 10 to 20 words	Continues using telegraphic speech	Continues using telegraphic speech combining three or four words
Prefers human voices	Acquires sounds of native language in babble	Adds *d*, *t*, *n*, and *w* to repertoire of babbling sounds	Demonstrates word comprehension skills	Engages in "jargon talk"	Able to combine three words	Speaks in complete sentences following word order of native language
Coos	Canonical, systematic consonant-vowel pairings; babbling occurs	Produces gestures to communicate, often by pointing	Waves good-bye	Engages in telegraphic speech by combining two words together	Talks, 25 percent of words being understandable	Displays effective conversational skills
Laughs	Participates in interactive games initiated by adults	May say *mama* or *dada* but does not connect words with parents	Speaks recognizable first word	Experiences a burst of language development	Refers to self by name	Refers to self as *me* or *I* rather than by name
Smiles and coos to initiate and sustain interactions with caregiver	Takes turns while interacting		Initiates familiar games with adults	Comprehends approximately 50 words	Joins three or four words into a sentence	Talks about objects and events not immediately present
					Comprehends approximately 300 words	Uses grammatical markers and some plurals
					Expressive language includes a vocabulary of approximately 250 words	Vocabulary increases rapidly, up to 300 words
						Enjoys being read to if allowed to participate by pointing, talking, and turning pages

*The developmental milestones listed are based on universal patterns of when various traits emerge. Because each child is unique certain traits may develop at an earlier or later age.

Developmental Milestones* (continued)

COGNITIVE DEVELOPMENT

Birth to Three Months	Four to Six Months	Seven to Nine Months	Ten to Twelve Months	Thirteen to Eighteen Months	Nineteen to Twenty-Four Months	Twenty-Five to Thirty-Six Months
Cries for assistance	Recognizes people by their voice	Enjoys looking at books with familiar objects	Solves sensorimotor problems by deliberately using schemas, such as shaking a container to empty its contents	Explores properties of objects by acting on them in novel ways	Points to and identifies objects on request, such as when reading a book, touring, etc.	Uses objects for purposes other than intended
Acts reflexively	Enjoys repeating acts, such as shaking a rattle, that produce results in the external world	Distinguishes familiar from unfamiliar faces	Points to body parts upon request	Solves problems through trial and error	Sorts by shapes and colors	Uses private speech while working
Prefers to look at patterned objects, bull's-eye, horizontal stripes, and the human face	Searches with eyes for source of sounds	Engages in goal-directed behavior	Drops toys intentionally and repeatedly looks in the direction of the fallen object	Experiments with cause-and-effect relationships such as turning on televisions, banging on drums, etc.	Recognizes self in photographs and mirror	Classifies objects based on one dimension, such as toy cars versus blocks
Imitates adults' facial expressions	Enjoys watching hands and feet	Anticipates events	Waves good-bye	Plays body identification games	Demonstrates deferred imitation	Follows two-step directions
Searches with eyes for sources of sounds	Searches for a partially hidden object	Finds objects that are totally hidden	Shows evidence of stronger memory capabilities	Imitates novel behaviors of others	Engages in functional play	Concentrates or attends to self-selected activities for longer periods of time
Begins to recognize familiar people at a distance	Uses toys in a purposeful manner	Imitates behaviors that are slightly different than those usually performed	Follows simple, one-step directions	Identifies family members in photographs	Finds objects that have been moved while out of sight	Points to and labels objects spontaneously, such as when reading a book
Discovers and repeats bodily actions such as sucking, swiping, and grasping	Imitates simple actions	Begins to show interest in filling and dumping containers	Categorizes objects by appearance		Solves problems with internal representation	Coordinates pretend play with other children
Discovers hands and feet as extension of self	Explores toys using existing schemas such as sucking, banging, grasping, shaking, etc.		Looks for objects hidden in a second location		Categorizes self and others by gender, race, hair color, etc.	Gains a nominal sense of numbers through counting and labeling objects in a set
						Begins developing concepts about opposites such as big and small, tall and short, in and out
						Begins developing concepts about time such as today, tomorrow, and yesterday

*The developmental milestones listed are based on universal patterns of when various traits emerge. Because each child is unique certain traits may develop at an earlier or later age.

Developmental Milestones* (continued)

SOCIAL DEVELOPMENT

Birth to Three Months	Four to Six Months	Seven to Nine Months	Ten to Twelve Months	Thirteen to Eighteen Months	Nineteen to Twenty-Four Months	Twenty-Five to Thirty-Six Months
Turns head toward a speaking voice	Seeks out adults for play by crying, cooing, or smiling	Becomes upset when separated from a favorite adult	Shows a decided preference for one or two caregivers	Demands personal attention	Shows enthusiasm for company of others	Observes others to see how they do things
Recognizes primary caregiver	Responds with entire body to familiar face by looking at the person, smiling, kicking legs, and waving arms	Acts deliberately to maintain the presence of a favorite adult by clinging or crying	Plays parallel to other children	Imitates behaviors of others	Views the world only from own, egocentric perspective	Engages primarily in solitary or parallel play
Bonds to primary caregiver		Uses adults as a base for exploration, typically	Enjoys playing with siblings	Becomes increasingly aware of the self as a separate being	Plays contently alone or near adults	Sometimes offers toys to other children
Finds comfort in the human face	Participates actively in interactions with others by vocalizing in response to adult speech	Looks to others who are exhibiting signs of distress	Begins asserting self	Shares affection with people other than primary caregiver	Engages in functional play	Begins to play cooperatively with other children
Displays a social smile	Smiles at familiar faces and stares solemnly at strangers	Enjoys observing and interacting briefly with other children	Begins developing a sense of humor	Shows ownership of possessions	Defends possessions	Engages in sociodramatic play
Is quieted by a voice	Distinguishes between familiar and unfamiliar adults and surroundings	Likes to play and responds to games such as patty-cake and peekaboo	Develops a sense of self-identity through the identification of body parts	Begins developing a view of self as autonomous when completing tasks independently	Recognizes self in photographs or mirrors	Wants to do things independently
Begins to differentiate self from caregiver		Engages in solitary play	Begins distinguishing boys from girls		Refers to self with pronouns such as *I* or *me*	Asserts independence by using "no" a lot
		Develops preferences for particular people and objects			Categorizes people by using salient characteristics such as race or hair color	Develops a rudimentary awareness that others have wants or feelings that may be different than their own
		Shows distress when in the presence of a stranger			Shows less fear of strangers	Makes demands of or "bosses" parents, guardians, and caregivers
						Uses physical aggression less and uses words to solve problems
						Engages in gender sterotypical behavior

*The developmental milestones listed are based on universal patterns of when various traits emerge. Because each child is unique certain traits may develop at an earlier or later age.

Developmental Milestones* (continued)

EMOTIONAL DEVELOPMENT

Birth to Three Months	Four to Six Months	Seven to Nine Months	Ten to Twelve Months	Thirteen to Eighteen Months	Nineteen to Twenty-Four Months	Twenty-Five to Thirty-Six Months
Feels and expresses three basic emotions: interest, distress, and disgust	Expresses delight	Responds to social events by using the face, gaze, voice, and posture to form coherent emotional patterns	Continues to exhibit delight, happiness, discomfort, anger, and sadness	Exhibits autonomy by frequently saying "no"	Expresses affection to others spontaneously	Experiences increase in number of fears
Cries to signal a need	Responds to the emotions of caregivers	Expresses fear and anger more often	Expresses anger when goals are blocked	Labels several emotions	Acts to comfort others in distress	Begins to understand the consequences of basic emotions
Quiets in response to being held, typically	Begins to distinguish familiar from unfamiliar people	Begins to regulate emotions through moving into or out of experiences	Expresses anger at the source of frustration	Connects feelings with social behaviors	Shows the emotions of pride and embarrassment	Learns skills for coping with strong emotions
Feels and expresses enjoyment	Shows a preference for being held by a familiar person	Begins to detect the meaning of others' emotional expressions	Begins to show compliance to caregivers' requests	Begins to understand complicated patterns of behavior	Uses emotion words spontaneously in conversations or play	Seeks to communicate more feelings with specific words
Shares a social smile	Begins to assist with holding a bottle	Looks to others for cues on how to react	Often objects to having playtime stopped	Demonstrates the ability to communicate needs	Begins to show sympathy to another child or adult	Shows signs of empathy and caring
Reads and distinguishes adults' facial expressions	Expresses happiness selectively by laughing and smiling more with familiar people	Shows fear of strangers	Begins eating with a spoon	May say "no" to something they want	Becomes easily hurt by criticism	Loses control of emotions and throws temper tantrums
Begins to self-regulate emotional expressions			Assists in dressing and undressing	May lose emotional control and have temper tantrums	Experiences a temper tantrum when goals are blocked, on occasion	Able to recover from temper tantrums
Laughs aloud			Acts in loving, caring ways toward dolls or stuffed animals, typically	Shows self-conscious emotions such as shame, guilt, and shyness	Associates facial expressions with simple emotional labels	Enjoys helping with chores such as cleaning up toys or carrying grocery bags
Quiets self by using techniques such as sucking a thumb or pacifier			Feeds self a complete meal when served finger foods	Becomes frustrated easily		Begins to show signs of being ready for toileting
			Claps when successfully completes a task			Desires that routines be carried out exactly as has been done in the past

*The developmental milestones listed are based on universal patterns of when various traits emerge. Because each child is unique certain traits may develop at an earlier or later age.

ASSESSING DEVELOPMENT

"All children have the potential, albeit in different ways, to learn and to develop their own ideas, theories, and strategies. All children also have the right to be supported in these endeavors by adults. Teachers and parents, therefore, should observe and listen to them" (Gandini & Goldhaber, 2001, p. 125).

Assessment is the process of observing, listening, recording, and documenting behavior in order to make decisions about a child's developmental and, thus, educational needs. This process is applicable for an individual child, a small group, or an entire group of children. Your observation skills are the main tools needed for assessing development. By observing and listening, you will discover much about children's needs, interests, and abilities.

This is a simple process. Your eyes and ears are like a video camera capturing children's behaviors, language, attitudes, and preferences. Most of the time you should be examining the children's abilities on worthy and meaningful tasks that you have created. Thus, your assessments will be directly tied to the curriculum that you have planned and implemented. For example, you do this when interacting with an infant or when assisting a toddler who is busy "working" at an experience. In other words, this is a spontaneous process that is continuously occurring. Authentic assessment requires your focused attention and some additional time for documenting your observation. To assist you in this process, a checklist has been included in Appendix H. If you are caring for more than one child, reproduce a copy for each. Appendix I is a form for recording anecdotal records. This form will allow you to document behaviors and incidents not represented on the checklist.

You can also record the children's performance during an activity, using a camera to document behavior and abilities.

There are several reasons why caregivers and parents need to assess the development of young children. First, assessment tracks growth and development, noting progress and change over time, thereby providing evidence of learning and maturation. Each observation conducted by a parent or caregiver provides a "snapshot" of the child's development. Combining several snapshots over time provides a comprehensive composite of the changes in the child's growth and development. These changes can be in one of three directions. Typically, children's growth and development follow a predictable sequence. That is, infants coo before they babble. Likewise, they produce a social smile before they are able to wave good-bye. Children can also continue working on the same skills. For example, they may spend several weeks or even months working on picking up objects with their thumbs and fingers. Finally, children can regress in their development. Although this happens infrequently, it can occur in times of great stress. For example, a toddler who had demonstrated proficiency at using a spoon at mealtime may revert back to using fingers to eat nonfinger foods.

Second, assessment provides insight to children's styles, interests, and dispositions. This information is invaluable in determining the correct level of responsiveness by parents and caregivers. It is much easier to meet a child's needs when you understand, for example, that the infant has difficulty transitioning from one activity to another. Knowing this assists you in preparing the infant for the next component of your daily routine, such as eating lunch.

Third, assessment data provides you with information regarding the normalcy of children's growth and development. This information directly impacts the experiences you create for the children. You should plan a balance of activities that support, enhance, and foster all areas of development. Some activities should be repetitious and represent developmental tasks that a child has accomplished yet still shows interest in and enjoys. Other activities should be a continuation of developmental tasks that the child is currently mastering. Still other activities should stimulate the child's development by requiring a higher skill level, thereby providing a challenge. At these times, children may need more adult support and assistance for scaffolding their learning as well as building their confidence as competent learners.

Fourth, developmental data must be gathered for effectively communicating the child's development with others. For example, if you are caring for children other than your own, you could discuss their progress with their parents or guardians. Likewise, if you are a parent, you will want to share this information with your child's caregiver, your significant other, or your child's pediatrician. Then, too, you may want to compile a portfolio or scrapbook containing a developmental checklist, photographs, videotapes, artwork, and other documents representing the child's growth and development.

Finally, assessment must be conducted to ensure that data is gathered for all areas of development. People have different biases and values. As a result, they may overlook or slight one area of development because of selective attention. If all areas are not assessed, experiences, toys, and equipment provided for children may not meet their developmental needs.

To undertake effective assessment, you will want to compile the data you collect into a meaningful form. The format you choose will depend on how you intend to use the data (Helm, Beneke, & Steinheimer, 1998). For example, if you wish to communicate with others about learning that occurred during a specific activity, you could display the artifacts collected, the photographs taken, and the dialogue transcribed while the children were working. If working in an early childhood program, this information could be displayed on a two-dimensional panel (see Appendix J) or a three-dimensional "Look at

What I Did Table." Moreover, to communicate about one child's current level of development, you might want to create a portfolio containing significant artifacts, such as a developmental checklist, anecdotal records, running records, photographs, and videotapes.

RESPECTING INFANTS

Respect. Regard. Honor. Value. These words are seldom used to describe very young children. Yet, these are traits or characteristics that are desired and valued in older children and adults. How better to teach such traits than to model them to infants from the very beginning? Respect must be demonstrated in your behaviors. More importantly, respect for infants must be something that emanates from inside of you. You have to believe that infants are worthy of your time and attention as individuals, because a respectful relationship is vital to all aspects of child development. For example, when infants are respected, they learn to trust that adults can be counted on to meet their needs. This foundation of trust allows them to actively explore their environment during toddlerhood. Hence, trust leads to learning about the world and the toddler's place in it.

It may seem hard to demonstrate respect to infants because we are unaccustomed to thinking about very young children in this manner. However, it is not difficult. Respect means believing in the children's abilities to explore, solve problems, or cause events to happen in their world. It also means setting and enforcing clear boundaries for behavior.

COMMUNICATING WITH INFANTS

Parents and caregivers play a vital role in helping children master communication and language skills. Listen to the infant-directed speech people use while interacting with and speaking to infants. Originally, this speech was referred to as "motherese"; now it is called "parentese." This type of speech involves speaking slowly and exaggerating changes both in intonation and pitch.

When people use parentese while speaking to an infant, the higher pitch and slower pace capture the child's attention. Then, too, the careful enunciation and simplified style and meanings make the speech easier for the child to understand. By emphasizing one word in a sentence, the adult helps to provide a focal point for the child. When speaking parentese, adults consciously reinforce the infant's role in the conversation by encouraging turn taking and responding to the child's utterances. The following example illustrates the components of parentese:

> Caregiver: *"Look at the kitteeee."*
> Infant responds by cooing: *"Ahhhhh."*
> Caregiver: *"The kitty is black."*
> Infant responds by cooing: *"Ahhhhh."*

> Caregiver: *"The cat is eating now."*
> Infant responds by cooing: *"Ohhhh."*
> Caregiver: *"Yes, you knew the cat was hungry."*

Common features of parentese are highlighted in the following table:

Common Features of "Parentese"

Producing Sounds
- Exaggerates intonation and uses higher pitch
- Moves frequently between high and low pitches, occasionally whispers
- Enunciates more clearly
- Emphasizes one or two words in a sentence
- Parrots a child's pronunciation, correct or incorrect

Simplifying Meanings
- Substitutes simple words for more complicated ones: moo moo for cow
- Uses diminutives: doggy for dog
- Labels objects according to simplest category: bird for parrot
- Repeats words invented by child: baba for bottle

Modifying Grammar
- Simplifies sentences grammatically to use short sentences: daddy go
- Uses nouns in lieu of pronouns: mommy helping Jeffrey
- Uses plural pronouns, if spoken: We drink our bottle

Interacting with a Child
- Focuses on naming objects, sounds, or events in the immediate environment
- Asks and answers own questions
- Uses questions more than statements or commands
- Pauses to allow for turn taking
- Repeats own utterances
- Responds to the child's utterances through repeating, expanding, and recasting

(Baron, 1992; Snow, 1998; Zigler & Stevenson, 1993)

Once young children begin understanding language, they begin using it. Language comprehension occurs before production. In the beginning, new words emerge slowly, then suddenly there is a burst. Nouns are acquired more rapidly than verbs. Children's first words focus on their body parts, toys, clothing, and words for social interaction such as *bye-bye* and *hello*. After developing and expressing a repertoire of single words, between 18 months and 2 years of age, children begin to combine words to make two-word phrases for communicating.

Kratcoski and Katz (1998) offer some guiding principles that can be used to support the children's language growth including:

♡ Use simple sentences.

♡ Speak slowly and clearly.

♡ Vary your tone/expression to emphasize key words.

♡ Use concrete vocabulary.

♡ Build from the child's utterance/phrase.

♡ Follow the child's topic of interest.

♡ Try to "comment" more than question. (p. 31)

Likewise, you need to:

♡ Provide the child with labels for objects, feelings, ideas, colors, and shapes.

♡ Give the child an opportunity to learn vocabulary in meaningful ways, and provide new objects and experiences to expand the child's language.

♡ Expose the child to a variety of books, catchy rhymes, and music.

♡ Connect the child's actions, ideas, and emotions with words.

♡ Engage in verbal interactions focusing on the child's interest. Prompt the child either by asking questions or creating a situation that requires a response.

♡ Engage the child in problem solving.

♡ Provide toys and household items that stimulate the child to talk.

RESPONDING TO INFANT BEHAVIORAL STATES

An infant's cues are important. Infants experience seven different behavioral states that caregivers need to recognize. Each behavioral state is characterized by differences in facial expressions, muscle tone, and alertness. Following birth, the newborn has irregular states. Predictable patterns, however, emerge within a few weeks. Additionally, newborns spend the majority of their day, between 16 and 20 hours, sleeping. As the baby grows and develops, the amount of sleep time decreases. Accordingly, the amount of time the infant is awake begins increasing. When this occurs, you will need to spend more time interacting with the child. The table above provides valuable information for recognizing the seven behavioral states. Study it carefully to be able to respond to the infant's cues.

Providing stimulation and the timing of interactions is important. Infants should not be interrupted or stimulated during regular, irregular, or periodic sleep or drowsiness. Rather, caregivers should observe for quiet alert periods. During this state, the infant exhibits a relaxed face and bright, focused eyes that are fully open. The child's activities are slight. Typically, the infant's hands will be open, with arms bent at the elbows and fingers extended.

SOOTHING INFANTS

When infants are crying, the caregiver should respond immediately. This reaction is important because children need to experience predictable and consistent care. Such care results in learning to trust, which is the foundation for later social-emotional development. Furthermore, responding promptly to the cries of infants is vital to the development of language and communica-

INFANT BEHAVIORAL STATES AND APPROPRIATE ADULT RESPONSES

State	Facial Expression	Action	Adult Response
Regular Sleep	Eyes closed and still; face relaxed	Little movement; fingers slightly curled, thumbs extended	Do not disturb
Irregular Sleep	Eyes closed, occasional rapid eye movement; smiles and grimaces	Gentle movement	Do not disturb
Periodic Sleep/ Drowsiness	Alternates between regular and irregular sleep; eyes open and close or remain halfway open; eyes dull/glazed	Less movement than in irregular sleep; hands open and relaxed, fingers extended	Do not disturb; Pick up if drowsiness follows sleeping; do not disturb if drowsiness follows awake periods
Quiet Alert	Bright eyes, fully open; face relaxed; eyes focused	Slight activity; hands open, fingers extended, arms bent at elbow; stares	Talk to infant; present objects; perform any assessment
Waking Activity	Face flushed; less able to focus eyes than in quiet alert state	Extremities and body move; vocalizes, makes noises	Interact with infant; provide basic care
Crying	Red skin; facial grimaces; eyes partially or fully open	Vigorous activity; crying vocalizations; fists are clenched	Pick up immediately; try to identify source of discomfort and remedy it; soothe infant

Adapted from Kostelnik et al. (2002)

tion skills. This teaches children that through communication their needs will be met.

Many caregivers worry that promptly responding to infants' cries will result in spoiling them. Current research suggests this is not true. In fact, some studies found that promptly responding to the cries of very young infants results in less crying at later stages of development (Zigler & Stevenson, 1993). The infants, in essence, have learned to trust that their communication results in signaling their caregivers.

The following table provides suggestions for soothing infants, including reasons for their effectiveness:

Soothing Crying Infants: Techniques and Reasons for Effectiveness

Technique	Reasons for Effectiveness
Lift baby to your shoulder and rock or walk	Provides a combination of physical contact, upright posture, and motion

Technique	Reasons for Effectiveness
Wrap tightly in a blanket	Restricts movement while increasing warmth
Offer a fist or pacifier	Provides pleasurable oral stimulation
Talk softly or provide a rhythmic sound such as a ticking clock or whirling fan	Reminds child of mother's heart-beat heard while in the uterus
Provide gentle rhythmic motions such as a short walk in a stroller or a ride in a swing	Lulls an infant to sleep
Massage the infant's body with continuous, gentle strokes	Relaxes the infant's muscles

INTERPRETING NONVERBAL CUES

Developing a social relationship with children is paramount and dependent on your ability to interpret their behaviors. This requires careful observation. You will study children's nonverbal behavioral cues. To illustrate, if the child is looking at you face-to-face, this behavior can be interpreted as being fully engaged. When this occurs, continue the interaction. However, if the child lowers the head, it is time to stop. The following table will provide you with some ways to interpret infants' behaviors and facial expressions:

Infant Gaze and Social Meaning to Caregivers

Position and Expression	Typical Interpretation
Face-to-face, sober	Fully engaged, intent
Face-to-face, smiling	Pleased, interested
Head turned slightly away	Maintaining interest; interaction too fast or too slow
Complete head rotation	Uninterested; stop for a while
Head lowered	Stop
Rapid head rotation	Dislikes something
Glances away, tilts head up; partial head aversion	Stop or change strategy
Head lowered, body limp	Has given up fighting off overstimulation

Source: Kostelnik et al. (2002)

If you fail to recognize the child's cues, the infant may become overstimulated. Overstimulation can result from interactions that are too intense. Noises or voices that are too loud can also contribute to overstimulation. When overstimulation occurs, infants protect themselves by changing from one state to another. Because there can be a rapid fluctuation between states, the goodness of fit between the child's state, the caregiver, and the environment is important. When children signal changes in state, alter your behavior immediately. Cease the interaction even without completing the activity. Of course, when the child signals readiness, the activity can be reintroduced.

APPLYING THIS BOOK

This book can be a wonderful companion when working with infants. To use it effectively, you will need to begin by reviewing the developmental norms and assessments. After this, you can use the checklist in Appendix I to begin gathering and documenting data. Once you have collected this developmental data, evaluate it to determine each child's needs, interests, and abilities. At this point, you are ready to begin searching for activities in this book that provide a balance of experiences to support, enhance, and foster all developmental areas.

When undertaking this process, you will need to narrow your selection of activities to prevent overstimulating the child(ren) in your care. This minimizes your preparation time and the amount of materials and equipment required; hence, you will have more energy to expend while interacting with the child(ren) in your care.

While working with infants, questions often arise. To support you, a list of resources related to infants has been included in Appendix G. You may discover these resources can be very useful in supporting your role as a caregiver.

We hope you enjoy reading and implementing the activities in this book as much as we did developing them. We leave you with this thought:

For a baby, those early weeks and months of growth, understanding, and reasoning can never be brought back to do over again. This is not the rehearsal. This is the main show. (Irving Harris)

Section II

Promoting Optimal Development in Infants

BIRTH to THREE MONTHS

FOUR to SIX MONTHS

PHYSICAL

LANGUAGE & COMMUNICATION

COGNITIVE

SOCIAL

EMOTIONAL

Physical Development

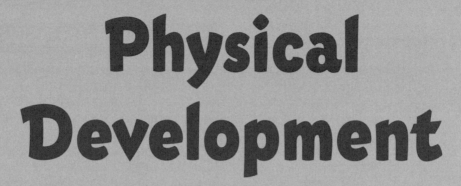

BIRTH to THREE MONTHS

DEVELOPMENTAL AREA: **Physical**

Rattle Time

PHYSICAL

Child's Developmental Goals

✓ To practice the grasping reflexes

✓ To refine eye-hand coordination skills

MATERIALS:
- ❑ 3 rattles of different sizes and sounds
- ❑ 3 eighteen-inch strips of elastic
- ❑ 6 diaper pins
- ❑ Infant crib
- ❑ Blanket or mat
- ❑ Masking tape

PREPARATION:
♡ Secure the rattles to the infant's crib. Begin by attaching one end of each piece of elastic around the center of each rattle with a diaper pin. After the rattles are attached, secure the other ends of the elastics to the bottom of the infant's crib with diaper pins. Adjust the elastics so that the infant can easily reach the rattles. Make sure the elastic is long enough so the rattle can be brought to the infant's mouth once it is "caught."

♡ Place the blanket halfway under the crib.

♡ Make sure you can continuously view the infant.

NURTURING STRATEGIES:
1. Lay the infant faceup on the blanket with the legs directly under the crib to allow easy viewing of the rattles.
2. Shaking the rattles may encourage the infant to attempt to swipe and grab them.
3. Provide positive reinforcement when the infant successfully makes contact with one of the rattles. For example, say:
   "Olivia, you did it! You are playing with the rattle. Listen to the rattle."
4. Continue the interaction by making such comments as:
   "Do it again!"
   "Olivia, touch this rattle."
5. Continue encouraging the infant to shake the rattle by making comments such as:
   "Can you shake the rattle?"

VARIATION:
♡ Suspending other infant toys that can be grasped may add interest. Examples include rubber floating toys and small stuffed animals.

☀ Highlighting Development

The newborn's distance vision is blurred. It is 10 to 30 times poorer than that of most adults. Thus, the visual acuity of an infant is about the same as adults who wear corrective glasses or contact lenses (Feldman, 1998).

An infant's visual system will not develop unless it is exercised. Babies can see at birth, although they cannot focus both eyes on a single object. Focusing distance is 8 to 10 inches. Therefore, the human face is a newborn's favorite "toy."

The ability to see, however, improves with age. By about one year of age, babies can see about as clearly as adults.

ADDITIONAL INFORMATION:
♡ Whenever possible, use the child's name. Then, too, use your voice and facial expressions to convey your enthusiasm.

♡ Checking the rattles for sharp edges and construction defects is important. Because rattles contain small pieces, they need to be replaced periodically due to normal wear and tear. To avoid a choking hazard, dispose of worn or defective rattles immediately.

♡ Rattle games foster the coordination of the infant's senses; the eyes and ears begin working together.

♡ When a rattle is placed in a newborn infant's palm, an automatic grasp reflex will occur.

 After closing diaper pins, always secure them by wrapping them with masking tape.

 Closely observe infants who are interacting with rattles. To help consumers choose safe toys for children under age three, the U.S. Consumer Product Safety Commission has set part-size standards. The ends of the rattle must be greater than 1⅜ inches in diameter to be safe for infants.

 Appendix B has additional criteria for selecting materials and equipment. Appendix C includes a list of materials and equipment for infants and toddlers.

 Whenever pillows or blankets are used, constant supervision is necessary to prevent the possibility of suffocation.

PHYSICAL

Lift Up and See

Child's Developmental Goals

✓ To strengthen upper-body muscles

✓ To practice lifting head

MATERIALS:

❑ 1 or 2 interesting infant toys

❑ Blanket or mat

PREPARATION:

♡ Select an area that you can constantly supervise. Spread the blanket out.

NURTURING STRATEGIES:

1. Lay the infant facedown on the blanket.
2. Talk about each toy as you place it in front of the infant. For example, say:
   "Taye, you like rattles. Here is a blue rattle. Look at it."
3. Pause. Observe the infant's efforts in lifting the head and shoulders.
4. Periodically observe the infant's attempts, accomplishments, and interests. Provide encouragement or positive reinforcement as necessary. Say, for example:
   "Look at the stuffed bunny, Taye."
   "You are looking at the bunny."

VARIATION:

♡ Propping open a favorite book, shaking a rattle, moving a puppet, or snapping your fingers to gain the infant's attention can provide variety. Encourage infants to raise their upper body; by doing so, they can have a better look at their surroundings.

Highlighting Development

Crying is a form of communication for the infant. It is a reflexive reaction to discomfort. Infants may cry because of pain, hunger, restlessness, boredom, and overstimulation.

Observe infants closely while interacting for signs of overstimulation since they cannot physically remove themselves from the situation. When this occurs, they may cry, withdraw, tune out, or drop off to sleep. If the child exhibits any of these behaviors, it is time to stop the activity.

ADDITIONAL INFORMATION:

♡ Trying new motor skills is not only strenuous, it can also be frustrating for infants. You might need to remain close to the infant. This will help prevent the infant from becoming upset or even distressed. In addition to becoming frustrated, infants tire easily.

♡ Readily respond to the child's cues or signals. When children receive responsive care, they are more likely to feel secure with their caregiver and in their environment.

♡ Babies also get bored when repeatedly shown the same thing. For this reason, you periodically need to change their visual stimulation to prevent boredom.

♡ The critical window of opportunity for developing vision is from birth to six months of age.

 Ensure the child's safety. Check the U.S. Consumer Safety Commission's Web site located at www.cpsc.gov to make sure that no toys you are using have been recalled.

 Whenever pillows or blankets are used, constant supervision is necessary to prevent the possibility of suffocation.

Wind Chime Stretch

Child's Developmental Goals

✓ To practice reaching and stretching the arm muscles
✓ To develop eye-hand coordination skills

MATERIALS:

❑ Wind chimes producing soft noise
❑ Tree or support structure
❑ Wool yarn
❑ Blanket or mat

PREPARATION:

♡ Select a flat, grassy area under a tree or support structure. Secure the wind chime from the structure with the yarn so that it is approximately ½ to ¾ feet from the ground. Adjust the height of the wind chime so that the infant has to stretch to reach it while lying on her back.

NURTURING STRATEGIES:

1. Lay the infant faceup on the blanket.
2. Encourage the infant to move the wind chime by saying:
   "Maya, look at me. I'm moving the chime. Can you move the chime?"
3. Reinforcing your words with actions may be necessary. If so, take the child's arm and move the chimes. Explain what is happening by saying, *"You moved the chime, Maya."*
4. Continue providing positive reinforcement and encouragement for the infant by saying: *"You did it! You moved the chime. You made a pretty sound. Listen. Do it again, Maya."*

 Highlighting Development

At birth, infants lie in a curled-up position similar to that of lying in the womb. They move their limbs in an uncontrolled, jerky manner. Over time, the brain refines the child's circuits, and motor skill development moves from gross to fine in two distinct patterns. First, motor control of the head comes before control of the arms, trunk, and legs. This developmental pattern is referred to as cephalo-caudal. Second, control of the head, trunk, and arms precedes control of fingers and feet. That is, growth occurs on a proximodestal pattern. Because of this, an infant's arms are small in proportion to the body trunk. Likewise, the hands and fingers are small in proportion to the arm.

VARIATIONS:

♡ Exercising leg muscles is important. Placing the wind chime over the infant's legs can promote the development of leg muscles.
♡ This activity can be adapted for use indoors.

ADDITIONAL INFORMATION:

♡ Choosing the wind chime is important to the success of this activity. Select a chime that makes soft, gentle noises; the infant may be more likely to engage in the activity.

 Carefully inspect the wind chime to ensure the small parts are securely attached.

Whenever pillows or blankets are used, constant supervision is necessary to prevent the possibility of suffocation.

Outside Tummy Time

Child's Developmental Goals

✓ To practice the grasping reflex

✓ To develop muscle coordination skills

MATERIALS:

❑ Blanket or mat

❑ Pillow that is at least 1 foot square

❑ 2 or 3 toys of interest

PREPARATION:

♡ Select a flat area and spread out the blanket.

♡ Place the pillow in the center of the blanket.

NURTURING STRATEGIES:

1. Lay the infant facedown on top of the pillow so that the upper body is supported by the pillow. This will free up the infant's arms and hands for exploration.

2. While placing each toy in front of the infant within reach, describe it for the child. Say, for example:

   "Here is your favorite toy, Peter. The black and white zebra is right here."

3. Encourage the infant to play with the toys. For example, say:

   "Reach out and grab it."

   "You can play with it."

4. Provide positive reinforcement when the infant attempts to or actually does play with a toy. Make such comments as:

   "Peter, you are holding the zebra."

☀ Highlighting Development

During the first three months, expect rapid development in hand and arm movements. The hand is clenched into a fist. Typically, the thumb is curled inside the fingers. When the hand comes in contact with the mouth, the child will typically suck it. This is comforting.

If you open the fingers and place a rattle in the palm, the infant will automatically grasp it. At two months of age, an infant can grasp a rattle briefly. By three months, an infant begins swiping at objects in the line of vision, but frequently misses.

In addition, infants grasp objects differently than toddlers, older children, or adults. First, infants look at objects, look at the hands, look back at the object, and proceed to move their hand to meet the object.

VARIATION:

♡ Suspending sun catchers will provide something interesting to look at when the infant raises up.

ADDITIONAL INFORMATION:

♡ This activity is good for infants who are just learning to lift their heads because it provides them with a break from this task. They are then able to use their energy to explore objects with their hands and mouths.

♡ At birth, touch is one of the most highly developed sensory systems. Touch is one of the ways infants gain information about their world.

 Whenever pillows or blankets are used, constant supervision is necessary to prevent the possibility of suffocation.

DEVELOPMENTAL AREA: **Physical**

Textured Mat

Child's Developmental Goals

✓ To explore different textures

✓ To strengthen upper-body muscles

MATERIALS:

☐ 4 identical-size pieces of carpet of different textures such as Berber or shag (include something soft, bumpy, smooth, and cushiony)

☐ Carpet thread, fishing line, or duct tape

☐ Upholstery needle

PREPARATION:

♡ Sew or tape together four pieces of carpet to make one large block.

♡ Select an area that you can constantly supervise. Clear this area, if needed, and spread out the textured mat.

NURTURING STRATEGIES:

1. While touching the infant's hand to each section, describe how the mat feels. For example, say:
   "Kenya, this part is soft."
   "This part is rough."
2. Lay the infant facedown on the textured mat.
3. Encourage the infant to explore the mat by making comments such as:
   "Kenya, you're touching the soft part."
   "Your hand is on the rough part."
4. Periodically reposition the mat so that all of the different textures are under the infant's hands.

☼ Highlighting Development

An infant's brain is unfinished at birth. Hence, infants need environmental stimulation. Frequent repetition of physical, intellectual, and emotional experiences helps promote the growth of a healthy brain. Through these experiences, the infant's brain becomes "wired."

VARIATION:

♡ Use mats that are commercially available. Some of these are see-through vinyl mats in which different objects float when the mat is filled with water. Because these mats can be filled with cold water, they are especially nice to use on hot summer days.

ADDITIONAL INFORMATION:

♡ Closely observe infants' reactions to the mat. They might not like the feeling of all the different textures. Move them around as needed.

♡ As infants develop the coordination to raise their heads and shoulders, you will observe the emergence of grabbing at the carpet or material under their hands. Hence, this experience provides practice for the grasping reflexes.

PHYSICAL

Lovin' Rubbin'

Child's Developmental Goals

✓ To develop awareness of body parts

✓ To coordinate seeing and touching

MATERIALS:

❑ Baby lotion

❑ Bath towel

❑ Changing table

PREPARATION:

♡ Check the changing table to ensure baby lotion is readily available.

NURTURING STRATEGIES:

1. This experience can be introduced after changing a diaper while the infant is lying on the changing table.

2. Place a quarter-size dab of lotion on one of your hands. Warm the lotion by rubbing your hands together before applying it on the infant.

3. Rub lotion on infant's chest, back, belly, arms, legs, hands, feet, fingers, toes, etc.

4. While rubbing on the lotion, talk about the body part you are touching. For example, say:
   "I'm putting lotion on Juan's feet and toes. How many toes do you have? 1, 2, 3, . . . 10. Yes, Juan has 10 toes!"
   In this situation, counting fosters the development of rhythm. This is important for language development.

5. When you are finished applying the lotion, dress the child.

☼ Highlighting Development

Infants need exposure to warm and positive relationships with their world. Through their senses—touching, smelling, hearing, seeing, and tasting—children experience relationships. These relationships affect how the infant's brain is wired, thereby shaping subsequent learning and behavior (Shore, 1997).

VARIATION:

♡ Doing this activity before nap time may help the infant to relax.

ADDITIONAL INFORMATION:

♡ When applying the lotion, use soft, gentle strokes. This type of stroking helps the infant to focus on the body part that is being touched at that time.

♡ If the child makes a sound like a gurgle or coo, move closer to the infant. Place your face close to the infant's so that you are seen. While smiling, repeat the infant's sound, thereby promoting language development.

DEVELOPMENTAL AREA: **Physical**

I'm Gonna Get Your Tummy!

PHYSICAL

Child's Developmental Goals

✓ To develop awareness of body parts
✓ To explore using the sense of touch

MATERIALS:

❑ Blanket, mat, or infant seat

PREPARATION:

♡ Select an area that you can constantly supervise. If needed, clear this area, and then place a blanket, mat, or infant seat there.

NURTURING STRATEGIES:

1. Lay the infant faceup on the blanket or mat. If using an infant seat, securely restrain the infant in the seat with the safety strap.
2. Begin the game by "walking" your index and pointer fingers up the infant's legs toward the abdomen while saying:
   "I'm gonna get your tummy, Adriana."
   Smile while playing this game. Because infants imitate, your expression should elicit a smile from the child.
3. When you get to the infant's tummy, tickle it! Hopefully, the infant will be showing signs of enjoying the activity such as smiling at this point.
4. Talk about the infant's reactions to the game. For example, comment:
   "Adriana, you like this game. You smiled when I got your tummy."
   "You're having fun!"
5. Repeat the activity as long as the infant shows signs of enjoying it, such as maintaining eye contact or smiling.

☼ Highlighting Development

The infant's physical development is rapid during this period. Changes in shape, size, and body proportions are occurring almost on a daily basis (Zigler & Stevenson, 1993). To illustrate, observe the infant's legs. They are becoming stronger and more active. Also, they are moving from the newborn position of curling inward to a straightened position.

VARIATION:

♡ Pretending to get different body parts, such as the infant's chin or toes, provides further information about the body.

ADDITIONAL INFORMATION:

♡ Pay close attention to the infants' cues. When infants are overstimulated or finished with the activity, they will let you know by doing things such as averting their eyes or even turning their entire head away from you. Often, infants will even cry when wanting to avoid activities they dislike such as dressing or undressing.

 Whenever pillows or blankets are used, constant supervision is necessary to prevent the possibility of suffocation.

Language and Communication Development

BIRTH to THREE MONTHS

Reciting Nursery Rhymes

Child's Developmental Goals

✓ To develop expressive language skills

✓ To hear native language patterns

MATERIALS:

❑ Select a nursery rhyme for this activity. See the list of nursery rhymes in Appendix D. Consider a short, nonfantasy rhyme with familiar words. In addition, always choose rhymes with nonviolent themes.

PREPARATION:

♡ If you have memorized the words to your favorite nursery rhymes, no materials are needed. However, if you need a prompt, create a poster with the words to your favorite nursery rhyme and hang it up or place it by your side for quick reference. This teaching tool may also be an aid for other adults to reinforce this activity.

NURTURING STRATEGIES:

1. Hold the infant in a position allowing you to visually connect.
2. Recite the nursery rhyme. Use your voice and facial expressions as tools for communicating enthusiasm.
3. Observe the infant for signs of interest. Some signs are eye contact, vocalizations, or smiles. If the child is interested, try repeating the nursery rhyme or reciting a different one.

☀ Highlighting Development

The word *infant* is derived from Latin. It means "without speech" (Junn & Boyatzis, 1998). An infant's first cry is the beginning of language development. One-month-old infants may respond with small, throaty sounds and cries. By three months of age, infants begin communicating by chuckling, squealing, and cooing.

Infants have much they want to tell people in their world. At first, communication focuses on hunger, pain, or being wet. Gradually, language learning emerges out of duet or social exchange between the adult and infant.

VARIATION:

♡ Reciting your favorite story or fable is another way to promote language development.

ADDITIONAL INFORMATION:

♡ Repeated exposure to their native language is important for infants learning to speak. One way to do this is by reciting nursery rhymes and stories. These language facilitation experiences are especially useful activities when infants have not developed the muscles for holding up their own heads. While holding the infant and verbally interacting, you are fostering the development of language skills.

♡ The infant enjoys the closeness and warmth of being held.

Infant-Picture Stories

Child's Developmental Goals

✓ To develop expressive language skills
✓ To practice vocalizing

MATERIALS:

❏ Pictures or posters of infants
❏ Blanket or mat (optional)
❏ Pillow

PREPARATION:

♡ Hang the pictures or posters at the infant's eye level.
♡ Clear the area on the floor next to the pictures for the blanket. If desired, spread out the blanket and place a pillow on the blanket.

NURTURING STRATEGIES:

1. Prop the infant up on one side on a blanket using the pillow for support.
2. Gain the infant's attention by pointing to a picture. For example, say:
   "Clint, look at this picture of a baby."
3. Create a story about the picture. Paralleling the story with the life or daily routines of the infant you are talking to makes this task easier. For instance, say:
   "This is Erin. She loves to play with rattles. She shakes the rattles."
4. Reinforce any vocalizations the infant makes during the story. Make comments such as:
   "Wow! That's true. You also like rattles, Clint."
   Doing this will encourage the infant to take part in the "conversation."

☼ Highlighting Development

An infant can perceive and produce sounds from the moment of birth. Speak and observe the infant's behavior. The infant will move to the rhythm of your speech. When your speech becomes faster, the infant will move his legs and arms faster. Likewise, if your speech slows, the infant's motions also will slow down. Hint: When you want the child to relax or even sleep, speak quietly and slowly.

Infants between one and three months will begin cooing. These sounds are open, vowel-like, gurgling sounds. Listen. You will hear "oooh" and "aaah." While crying is a signal of distress, cooing signals happiness and contentment (Snow, 1998).

VARIATION:

♡ Post pictures on the wall at your eye level. Hold the infant and walk around the room while looking, commenting, and telling stories about the pictures.

ADDITIONAL INFORMATION:

♡ Infants are particularly interested in stories and pictures of other infants. Therefore, this activity can be used to foster the development of social skills in older infants.

 Whenever pillows or blankets are used, constant supervision is necessary to prevent the possibility of suffocation.

Rockin' the Day Away

Child's Developmental Goals

✓ To develop receptive language skills

✓ To practice communication skills

MATERIALS:

❑ Outside rocker or glider

PREPARATION:

♡ Observe the child to make sure she is in a responsive state.

NURTURING STRATEGIES:

1. While sitting in the rocker or glider, hold the infant in your lap so you both are facing the same direction.
2. While rocking, talk about the surrounding environment. You can discuss different objects as well as people that you can see. When talking, use as many descriptive words as possible. Comments might include:
   "Look at the little, red bird. It is sitting in the green pine tree."
3. Reinforce any vocalizations the infant makes. To illustrate, say:
   "Yes, the bird flew away."
   "Tell me more about the red bird."
   Doing this may encourage the infant to continue to take part in the "conversation."

☀ Highlighting Development

Adopt a parentese style to help the infant learn. This type of speech attracts babies' attention. To do this when speaking, place your face very close to the infant so that she is able to see you. To capture the infant's attention, use a high-pitched, rhythmic style and short utterances. Speak slowly and with careful enunciation. The parentese style will make it easier for the baby to hear individual sounds.

VARIATIONS:

♡ Repeat this activity inside before nap time. It may help the infant to relax.

♡ Singing rather than talking to the infant may be enjoyable for everyone.

ADDITIONAL INFORMATION:

♡ Periodically moving the rocker or glider to different locations will provide a new view of the world. As a result, there will be "new" things to look at and talk about.

Picture Book Time

Child's Developmental Goals

✓ To develop expressive language skills

✓ To engage in taking turns

MATERIALS:

❑ Black and white picture book

❑ Blanket or mat

PREPARATION:

♡ Clear an area and then spread out the mat or blanket.

♡ Prop open the book on the blanket or mat.

NURTURING STRATEGIES:

1. Place the infant faceup on the blanket.
2. Gain the infant's attention by looking in the child's eyes and saying:
   "Ridi, look at what I have. A book. Let's read it together."
3. "Read" the picture book to the infant. Pointing to the pictures and verbally identifying the object will assist the infant in connecting words with objects. While saying the word or describing what is on the page, "converse" with the infant.
4. To promote turn taking, ask questions such as:
   "Ridi, what is this?"
   Wait for a response.
5. Encourage the infant to continue responding by providing positive reinforcement to the vocalizations. Make comments such as:
   "You are right! It is a baby."
6. Closely observe the infant for signs of interest. When the infant begins to lose interest, stop reading. However, read the book a second or third time if the infant maintains interest.

Highlighting Development

When selecting pictures or toys, remember babies prefer patterns over solids. At birth, they prefer looking at black and white in a vertical stripe. Watch them search pictures and toys. Because fewer eye muscles are needed for scanning patterns horizontally, newborns use this method.

VARIATIONS:

♡ Allow the infant to "read" the book when you are finished. An infant will "read" the book by holding and mouthing it. Vinyl, cloth, or plastic books are especially good for this reason.

♡ Select a picture book with only colored pictures and no words. Create a story for the child about the objects in the book.

ADDITIONAL INFORMATION:

♡ Just like infants' play with other toys, they need the opportunity to explore books with their hands and mouths. Having several vinyl or plastic books available will allow you to substitute a clean book for a soiled book. To promote a healthy environment, infant toys should be sanitized as often as necessary, usually several times throughout the day.

 Avoid letting toys sit in the sun. They can become hot enough to burn the child.

Whenever pillows or blankets are used, constant supervision is necessary to prevent the possibility of suffocation.

DEVELOPMENTAL AREA: **Language & Communication**

The Lullaby Rub

Child's Developmental Goals

✓ To develop expressive language skills

✓ To hear native language patterns

MATERIALS:

❏ Select a short lullaby for this activity.

❏ If you have memorized the words to your favorite lullaby, no materials are needed. However, if you need a prompt, create a poster or "crib sheet" with the words to hang in the crib area for quick reference. This teaching tool may also be an aid for others who interact with the child.

PREPARATION:

♡ Observe the infant to determine the best time for introducing the lullaby rub.

NURTURING STRATEGIES:

1. Place the infant faceup in the crib.
2. While rubbing the infant's abdomen, look into the child's eyes and sing the lullaby you selected. Use your voice as a tool to soothe and communicate that it is time to sleep.
3. Repeat the lullaby as many times as necessary. Rubbing the infant's abdomen and singing the lullaby may help the infant to relax and, hopefully, promote sleep.

☀ Highlighting Development

The number of words children hear will affect their language development. The language children experience needs to be related to ongoing events in their lives. Consequently, the television will not produce the language-boosting effects for infants and toddlers that caregivers, siblings, or other adults can provide. For variety, you may supplement your voice with music recorded on compact discs or tapes.

VARIATION:

♡ Softly recite your favorite finger play or sing a song.

ADDITIONAL INFORMATION:

♡ Infants, like adults, sometimes need help relaxing before falling asleep. Singing, rubbing, or rocking are often soothing activities for infants.

Given the threat of Sudden Infant Death Syndrome, infants should be placed on their backs to sleep.

What Am I Doing?

Child's Developmental Goals

✓ To develop receptive language skills

✓ To engage in a conversation

MATERIALS:

None

PREPARATION:

♡ Observe the infant for times of alertness.

NURTURING STRATEGIES:

1. This activity works best during routine care times such as feeding.
2. Hold the infant so that you can visually connect with the child while preparing a bottle.
3. Talk about what you are doing. For example, say:
   "Carrie, I'm warming your bottle. You like warm bottles. Milk tastes good when it's warm."
4. Respond to the vocalizations or cries of the infant with conversation. To illustrate, comment:
   "You are very hungry. I'm warming the bottle for you. The milk will taste so good. It is almost done. You are so hungry!"

Highlighting Development

Reading an infant's subtle signs is an important tool for assessing behavior. When the child lies still with bright and wide eyes, the infant is probably in a state of enjoyment and is ready to interact. When this occurs, sing, look, talk, and read to the child. These interactions will stimulate the child's brain to make connections that are important to growth and later learning.

VARIATION:

♡ Talk about what the other people in the infant's environment are doing. This technique is most effective if another person is locating something for the infant you are working with. For example, say:
"Barbara is bringing your blanket. I forgot it. You need your blanket to sleep."

ADDITIONAL INFORMATION:

♡ Infants learn by repetition. By hearing caregivers talk about routine care or tasks, infants associate particular words with actions. This contributes to the development of their receptive language skills.

♡ The acquisition of language is one of the most remarkable accomplishments of early childhood. The beginnings of language focus on the interaction between caregiver and infant.

What Are You Doing?

Child's Developmental Goals

✓ To develop receptive language skills

✓ To participate in a conversation

MATERIALS:

None

PREPARATION:

♡ Observe the child's state of readiness. If the child is alert, introduce the activity.

NURTURING STRATEGIES:

1. This activity works best during routine care times such as preparation for napping.
2. Hold the infant so you can visually connect with the child while preparing the crib.
3. Talk about what the infant is experiencing. For example, say:

   "Logan, it's time for your nap. You are very tired. You keep rubbing your eyes. That tells me you need to sleep."
4. Respond to the vocalizations or cries of the infant with conversation. To illustrate, comment:

   "Logan, you are very sleepy. Your crib is ready now. You can enjoy a nice nap."

☼ Highlighting Development

Infants have a range of preferences, which may vary from child to child. Discover their likes and dislikes by observing them and experimenting. Like adults, children desire variety. Sometimes an energetic baby may prefer quiet and soothing interactions while a quiet baby may prefer more dramatic interactions.

VARIATION:

♡ Talk about what other children or people are doing.

ADDITIONAL INFORMATION:

♡ Talking about the routine care or tasks that are being experienced on a daily basis will help the infant to associate words with actions. Hence, describing the routine tasks can greatly increase the infant's receptive language skills.

♡ This activity can help soothe a child, as well as provide language stimulation.

Cognitive
Development

BIRTH to THREE MONTHS

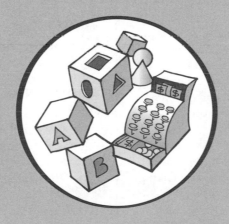

DEVELOPMENTAL AREA: **Cognitive**

Tugging the Towel

COGNITIVE

Child's Developmental Goals

✓ To practice the grasping reflex

✓ To gain voluntary control over reflexes

MATERIALS:

❑ Hand towel

❑ Blanket or mat

PREPARATION:

♡ Spread out the blanket or mat in an area that can be constantly supervised.

NURTURING STRATEGIES:

1. Lay the infant faceup on the blanket. Sitting in an upward position, move your legs into a "V" formation. You should be facing the infant. In addition, you should be able to comfortably bend over.

2. Roll the towel. Then gently pick up and place each of the infant's hands on to the towel. This will help to stimulate the infant's palmar grasp reflex. Hold on to the towel so that your hands are on the outside of both of the infant's hands.

3. Slowly pull your hands toward your body and gently raise the infant's shoulders from the blanket.

4. As you raise the infant, engage the child by talking. Describe what is happening. For example, say: *"Kayla, you pulled yourself up. What a strong baby!"*

5. Then lower the infant to the blanket or mat. Make sure to gently lay the infant's head down.

6. Repeat this activity until the infant signals a lack of interest.

☼ Highlighting Development

Infants make contact by signaling. Attentiveness is shown through visual tracking and looking into another's face (Kostelnik et al., 2002). Infants will also signal you when they finish an activity. They will cry, fuss, turn their heads away, or otherwise signal that they have completed this activity. By closely observing an infant, you will know when to stop. To soothe the child, cuddle, rock, pat, or provide something for sucking.

VARIATION:

♡ Substitute your index fingers for the infant to hold on to instead of the towel.

ADDITIONAL INFORMATION:

♡ When selecting a towel, blanket, or mat, consider infants' preferences. Typically, they prefer bright colors and unusual, soft textures.

 Whenever pillows or blankets are used, constant supervision is necessary to prevent the possibility of suffocation.

COGNITIVE

Reach for It!

Child's Developmental Goals

✓ To practice eye-hand coordination skills

✓ To imitate a caregiver's behavior

MATERIALS:

❏ Mobile

PREPARATION:

♡ Suspend the mobile from the ceiling at a height that is comfortable for an adult to reach while holding an infant.

NURTURING STRATEGIES:

1. Carry the infant over to the mobile.
2. Touch the mobile with your hand and describe what is happening. Comments might include: *"I moved the mobile. I used my hand. Watch me."*
3. Invite the infant to imitate your actions by saying: *"Rashad, can you make the mobile move? Touch it with your hand. Push it. Swipe at it. Watch."*
4. Raise the infant up so that the swiping motions result in moving the mobile.
5. Praising the infant for moving the mobile, you might say: *"Rashad, good for you. You did it. You moved the mobile. You used your hand."*
6. Invite the infant to move the mobile again. Increase the challenge by positioning the infant so that the mobile is a little farther away.
7. Encourage the infant to move the mobile again. Comments might include: *"Rashad, reach. You can do it."* If the child moves the mobile, praise the accomplishment. If the infant's swipe misses the mobile, provide further encouragement.
8. If the infant continues swiping without touching the mobile, adjust your position by moving closer.

☀ Highlighting Development

Studies show infants usually look longer at a novel object than at a familiar object (Baillargeon, 1994). They need to be stimulated with things to look at such as other people, mobiles, stuffed toys, nonglass mirrors, etc. When stimulated, watch the infant's face freeze with intense interest. Observe. It is amazing how much interest infants can invest in a toy that appeals to their senses.

VARIATION:

♡ Suspending the mobile from a counter or table will encourage the infant to move it while lying on the floor. Increasing the distance between the mobile and the floor, once the infant has experienced success in moving the mobile, will provide a new challenge.

ADDITIONAL INFORMATION:

♡ Provide infants with positive reinforcement when they are engaging in activities. Also, use infants' names during activities. By doing so, they will learn to recognize it.

 For safety purposes, the string attaching the mobile to the ceiling must be strong enough to support the infant's weight.

DEVELOPMENTAL AREA: **Cognitive**

Touring in the Stroller

Child's Developmental Goals

✓ To enhance existing cognitive structures

✓ To integrate the senses of seeing and hearing

MATERIALS:

❑ Infant stroller

PREPARATION:

♡ This tour can be scheduled indoors or outdoors, depending on the weather and available space. If going outside, dress the infant appropriately for the weather. Remember, infants need outdoor stimulation as much as older children or adults.

NURTURING STRATEGIES:

1. Place the infant securely in the stroller using safety restraints.

2. Begin the tour by pushing the stroller and talking about what you see. For example, say:
   "Olga, there goes a car. It is moving fast."
   "Here is a flower. It is yellow."
   Continue communicating with the child by commenting on what you are seeing. Remember to focus on pointing out objects only at the infant's eye level.

3. Kneel down occasionally, look in the child's eyes to gain attention, and point out objects in the environment.

☀ Highlighting Development

A stimulating environment promotes growth of the infant's cognitive structures. For this to happen, caring, responsible adults need to introduce variations in the environment. The infant needs stimulation and responsiveness. In fact, the way parents, families, and other caregivers relate, respond, and mediate the infant's contact with the environment directly affects brain development (Shore, 1997).

VARIATIONS:

♡ Increase the number of children on the tour to add variety.

♡ If possible, take tours to various locations such as parks, grocery stores, zoos, etc. Invite older children to join you since they provide different types of stimulation.

ADDITIONAL INFORMATION:

♡ Always look at the tour through the eyes of an infant. There are so many new things to see! Be as descriptive as you can when talking. The sound of surprise in your voice when discovering something novel will assist in gaining the infant's attention.

♡ The rhythm, pattern, and sound of your voice contribute to the child's language development.

Bell Ringing

Child's Developmental Goals

✓ To experience the principle of cause and effect

✓ To develop existing cognitive structures

MATERIALS:

❑ Elastic band (length depends upon the size of the infant's hands)

❑ Large bell, a minimum of 2 inches in diameter

❑ Fishing line

❑ Blanket or infant seat

PREPARATION:

♡ Cut a piece of elastic band large enough so that it comfortably fits over the infant's hand. Once placed on the infant's arm, it should not leave a mark on the skin. Sew the elastic ends together using a piece of fishing line. Then tightly secure the bell to the elastic band. Pull on the bell to ensure that it remains attached to the elastic.

NURTURING STRATEGIES:

1. Place the infant faceup on the blanket. Otherwise, secure the infant into the seat, fastening the safety restraint.

2. Place the elastic band with the bell on the infant's arm.

3. Gently shake the infant's arm, acting surprised when the bell makes a sound.
   "Andre, what was that? Listen. Can you make that sound again?"

4. Wait to see if infant repeats the movement. If it is repeated, provide positive reinforcement by making comments such as:
   "Andre, you are making a sound."
   If a noise is not made, shake the infant's arm again. Wait to see if the movement is repeated.

5. If there's no response, the infant probably is interested in something else right now. Try this experience again later.

☀ Highlighting Development

Infants gradually are beginning to note their effect on the world. Therefore, they need interactive experiences and some structure to their playtime. At this stage of development, the child loves people most of all. He enjoys responding to their facial expressions, listening to their voices, and being cuddled. In fact, the infant's preference for a toy is a human face.

VARIATION:

♡ Make an elastic band with a bell attached to fit the infant's leg.

ADDITIONAL INFORMATION:

♡ Whenever possible, reinforce words with actions. To illustrate, when saying the word *shake,* perform the action.

♡ Continue the activity as long as the infant is showing interest. Promptly remove the band if the infant appears frightened by the sound of the bell or the feel of the band.

 For safety purposes, use the paper core of a toilet paper roll to check the bell size. If the bell falls through, it is considered a choking hazard for infants.

 Whenever pillows or blankets are used, constant supervision is necessary to prevent the possibility of suffocation.

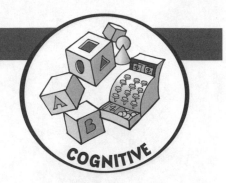

Infant Imitation

COGNITIVE

Child's Developmental Goals

✓ To imitate a caregiver's action

✓ To experience repetition of an action

MATERIALS:

None

PREPARATION:

♡ Observe the infant to note alertness.

NURTURING STRATEGIES:

1. This activity can occur any time when you are interacting with the infant throughout the day. However, an ideal time to introduce the activity would be during the diapering routine.
2. Closely listen to any sounds the infant makes (e.g., ooooo).
3. Imitate that sound by repeating what the infant said (e.g., ooooo).
4. Usually, the infant will repeat the sound again to continue the "conversation." When this happens, provide positive reinforcement in the form of praising or smiling. You could comment, for example:

    "We are talking to each other."

☼ Highlighting Development

According to new brain research, infants' brains rapidly develop from the moment of birth. Infants' optimal development is dependent on the experiences provided for them during the first three years of life. At birth, the brain stem, which controls vital wiring for breathing and the heartbeat, is completed. The connections in other parts of the brain's circuit are weak. These circuits govern emotions, language, math, music, and language. The circuits for governing emotions are some of the first circuits constructed. Therefore, the right kind of emotional stimulation is important (Shore, 1997).

VARIATIONS:

♡ Imitate an infant's facial expression, such as a frown or smile.

♡ Performing an action such as sticking out your tongue or saying "ahhh" with exaggerated movements while looking at the infant may also result in an "imitative" conversation. Sticking out the tongue is one of the first actions a child can imitate.

ADDITIONAL INFORMATION:

♡ Infants will tell you through their behavior when they have finished with an activity. They will cry, fuss, turn their heads away, fall asleep, or otherwise signal that they have had enough stimulation. To prevent the frustration of overstimulation, show sensitivity by closely observing and responding to an infant's signal.

COGNITIVE

Can You Follow Me?

Child's Developmental Goals

✓ To practice coordinating the senses of hearing and seeing

✓ To develop existing cognitive structures

MATERIALS:

❑ Blanket, mat, or infant seat

PREPARATION:

♡ Select an area that you can constantly supervise. Clear this area and spread out the blanket, mat, or infant seat.

NURTURING STRATEGIES:

1. Lay the infant faceup on the blanket or mat; otherwise, secure the infant in the seat with the safety restraint.
2. Gain the infant's attention by talking about what the infant can see. For example, say:
   "Maha, you are looking at me. Can you follow me? I'm going to move."
3. While continuing to talk, move your body out of the visual path to a different location near the infant such as to the side of the child.
4. Observe the infant's behavior. Did the infant move any part of her body to visually locate you again? If movement was detected, provide positive reinforcement. Comment by saying:
   "Maha, you can still see me. You moved your head to find me."
   If the infant did not respond, move back into her visual path to regain her attention.
5. Repeat steps 3 and 4 as long as the infant is interested in the activity.

☼ Highlighting Development

It is important to exercise both sides of the infant's body. Using a rattle, move the location of the sound equally to both the left and right side. Avoid moving the rattle behind the infant's head, which makes it difficult for the infant to experience success in locating you. Once infants have developed control of their neck and head muscles, the rattle can be moved behind their head.

VARIATION:

♡ Use a soft bell, drum, rattle, or musical instrument instead of your voice.

ADDITIONAL INFORMATION:

♡ Infants are learning to track and follow objects. As a result, they need experiences and interactions for practice to promote their optimum development.

♡ At birth, the auditory system is fairly well developed. This is not surprising because infants have had some practice in hearing before birth (Feldman, 1998).

 Whenever pillows or blankets are used, constant supervision is necessary to prevent the possibility of suffocation.

DEVELOPMENTAL AREA: Cognitive

Get Me If You Can!

Child's Developmental Goals

✓ To enhance coordination of the arm muscles

✓ To practice the grasping and sucking reflexes

MATERIALS:

❏ Blanket or mat

❏ 2 to 3 plastic, rubber, or fabric infant toys

❏ Pillow at least 1 foot square

PREPARATION:

♡ Select an area that you can constantly supervise. Clear this area and spread out the blanket or mat.

NURTURING STRATEGIES:

1. Lay the infant facedown on the blanket if he has acquired the skill of lifting the head and shoulders up from the surface. Lay the infant on one side and support the back with pillows if this skill is undeveloped.

2. Show the toys by placing them in the infant's visual track. Then begin verbally describing them. Say, for example:
   "Here is a rubber duck. You see the eyes. You can squeeze this."

3. Place these toys in the infant's visual path, but just beyond his reach.

4. Verbally encourage the infant to reach for the toys. For example, say:
   "Sean, get it. Stretch. You can do it. Reach for the duck."

5. When the infant touches a toy, provide positive reinforcement, such as:
   "You did it. You stretched and touched the rattle."
   Use your voice to share your enthusiasm.

6. Encourage the infant to grasp and suck the toy. To illustrate, say:
   "Sean, grab the rattle."
   "Put it in your mouth."

7. If the infant becomes upset or distressed because the toys are out of reach, move them closer.

☼ Highlighting Development

Infants can become frustrated, upset, and even distressed when they cannot reach something within their visual path. Some frustration can be a positive experience because it encourages them to think and explore different ways to solve their problems. However, pay close attention to the sound of their voice. Intervening and moving the toys closer may prevent infants from becoming too upset or distressed.

VARIATION:

♡ Use a ball or small, soft teddy bear to encourage the child's grasping behavior.

ADDITIONAL INFORMATION:

♡ Collect a variety of toys. If the infant does not show interest in one toy, try introducing another.

 Whenever pillows or blankets are used, constant supervision is necessary to prevent the possibility of suffocation.

Social
Development

BIRTH to THREE MONTHS

Where Are Your Toes?

SOCIAL

Child's Developmental Goals

✓ To develop a positive self-image
✓ To experience social interactions

MATERIALS:

None

PREPARATION:

♡ Select a song to sing, such as the one that follows, containing the child's name.

NURTURING STRATEGIES:

1. After diapering and before removing the infant from the changing table, sing the following song: (Tune: "The Farmer in the Dell")

   ♫ Where are *Rosa*'s toes?   (shrug shoulders)
   ♫ Where are *Rosa*'s toes?   (shrug shoulders)
   ♫ Hi Ho Hi Ho
   ♫ Here are *Rosa*'s toes.   (point to toes)

2. Substitute different body parts such as arms, hands, ears, legs, and fingers in the verse.
3. Continue singing this song as long as the infant shows interest by maintaining eye contact, smiling, etc.

☀ Highlighting Development

Babies can read your moods by the look on your face, the sound of your voice, and your interaction style. In addition, they imitate your moods. Therefore, if you appear sad, the baby will be sad. Likewise, if you are happy and energetic, chances are the baby will imitate your mood.

VARIATIONS:

♡ Sing about and point to your own body parts.
♡ Change the word *are* to *is* in the song. Then use the words *mouth, nose, hair, thumb,* and *knee*.

ADDITIONAL INFORMATION:

♡ This activity is most successful when the infant is in the quiet-alert stage of wakefulness. During this time, infants are most responsive and enjoy interacting with others.
♡ The most fascinating thing for an infant to observe is your face.

SOCIAL

Where Are You?

Child's Developmental Goals

✓ To form a positive self-image

✓ To develop self-identity

MATERIALS:

❑ Blanket, mat, or infant seat

PREPARATION:

♡ Select an area of the room that can be easily supervised. Spread out the blanket or place the infant seat in this area.

NURTURING STRATEGIES:

1. Lay the infant faceup on the blanket. Otherwise, securely place the child in an infant seat, fastening the safety restraint.
2. Gain the infant's attention by singing the following song:
   (Tune: "Where Is Thumbkin?")

   ♫ Where is *Marcus*? Where is *Marcus*?
   ♫ There he is. There he is.   (point to infant)
   ♫ How are you today, *Marcus*?
   ♫ Very well we hope so.
   ♫ Want to play? Want to play?

3. Stimulate the infant by talking about reactions to the song. For example, say:
   "What a smile! You liked that song, Marcus. Should we sing it again?"
4. Repeat the song as long as the infant seems interested and enjoys it. Check for signs of interest such as maintaining eye contact, smiling, or cooing.

☼ Highlighting Development

By three months of age, most infants will track sounds by turning their heads and gazing toward the source. Their brains are stimulated by hearing a variety of sounds. From this stimulation, new connections called "learning pathways" are formed. At the same time, existing connections are strengthened (Shore, 1997).

VARIATION:

♡ Move away from the infant to another part of the room. Repeat the song. Observe the infant's ability to track your voice.

ADDITIONAL INFORMATION:

♡ Infants love to hear songs, especially ones that include their names. Continue this activity as long as the infants' behaviors indicate pleasure or enjoyment. Infants convey disinterest by looking away, fussing, or crying when they are finished with an activity.

 Whenever pillows or blankets are used, constant supervision is necessary to prevent the possibility of suffocation.

DEVELOPMENTAL AREA: Social

Singing Good-Bye

SOCIAL

Child's Developmental Goals

✓ To develop self-identity

✓ To develop social interaction skills

MATERIALS:

None

PREPARATION:

♡ Observe the infant's state of consciousness to determine the level of responsiveness.

NURTURING STRATEGIES:

1. When a guest, sibling, or a child is departing, sing the following song:

    ♫ Good-bye *Terri*.
    ♫ Good-bye *Terri*.
    ♫ Good-bye *Terri*.
    ♫ We'll see you another day.

    (Rhonda Whitman, Infant-Toddler Specialist University of Wisconsin–Stout)

2. Foster social development by showing the infant how to wave good-bye. You could say, for example:
    "Watch me wave good-bye, Terri."
    Whenever necessary, reinforce your words with actions.

☀ Highlighting Development

Infants prefer an orderly, consistent, and predictable environment. They also become familiar with, like, and need routines. Routines help them develop a sense of security. Infants, like other children, are reassured when routines are associated with rituals and pleasurable feelings.

VARIATION:

♡ Sing this song to family members before they leave for the day.

ADDITIONAL INFORMATION:

♡ Singing this song consistently is important for both infants and adults.

What's Everyone Doing?

Child's Developmental Goals

✓ To develop social interaction skills

✓ To develop a self-identity

MATERIALS:

❑ Blanket, mat, or infant seat

PREPARATION:

♡ Select an area that you can constantly supervise. Clear this area and spread out the blanket or mat. If preferred, use the infant seat.

NURTURING STRATEGIES:

1. Lay the infant faceup on a blanket or mat. Otherwise, secure the child in the infant seat using the safety restraint.

2. Talk to the infant about where you are going to be working and what you will be doing. For example, comment:
   "Emilio, I'm by the sink. I'm making a bottle. You are hungry."

3. Observe the infant's interests and behavior. Talk about what the infant is looking at. For example, say:
   "Emilio, that is a poster of a baby. That baby is in the snow. The snow is cold."

4. If necessary, encourage the infant to look at other objects or people in the immediate environment. To illustrate, comment:
   "Look at Tommy push the balls. He is using his hands."

5. Provide positive reinforcement to acknowledge what the infant is looking at. For example, say:
   "Emilio, you are watching me. I am heating your bottle."

☀ Highlighting Development

Infants regulate their level of stimulation verbally and nonverbally. Observe them. Play with them in a way that lets you follow their lead. Move in when children want to play and pull back when they seem to have had enough stimulation. By following their lead, you are respecting their needs (Shore, 1997).

VARIATION:

♡ Provide a toy for the infant to hold while looking around the room. When people are not in sight, this will give the infant something to play with.

ADDITIONAL INFORMATION:

♡ Infants need constant supervision to promote their health and safety. However, this does not mean you have to be beside the infant the entire day. Observing and talking to the infant from another part of the room will meet his needs for security and safety.

 Whenever pillows or blankets are used, constant supervision is necessary to prevent the possibility of suffocation.

DEVELOPMENTAL AREA: **Social**

Welcome Song

SOCIAL

Child's Developmental Goals

✔ To begin the day positively

✔ To develop self-identity

MATERIALS:

None

PREPARATION:

♡ Observe the infant's state of consciousness to determine the level of responsiveness.

NURTURING STRATEGIES:

1. When a guest, family member, or child arrives, greet her by saying her name. For example, say: *"Good morning Ramona. How are you today?"*

2. Look at the child and sing the following song while waving:

   ♫ Hello *Ramon*a.
   ♫ Hello *Ramon*a.
   ♫ Hello *Ramon*a.
   ♫ We're so glad you're here.

(Rhonda Whitman, Infant-Toddler Specialist University of Wisconsin–Stout)

☼ Highlighting Development

During this stage, infants enjoy being held and drawn into social interactions with people in their environment. Unlike in subsequent stages, they do not discriminate their primary caregiver from other people they might interact with.

VARIATION:

♡ Sing the song in the Singing Good-Bye activity in this section.

ADDITIONAL INFORMATION:

♡ Infants love to hear songs, especially ones that include their names.

♡ Singing this song is important for infants. They become familiar with, like, and need routines. Routines help them develop a sense of security.

SOCIAL

Waking Up

Child's Developmental Goals

✓ To develop a sense of trust

✓ To acquire a positive sense of self

MATERIALS:

None

PREPARATION:

♡ Listen for the infant's cries or movements that indicate wakefulness.

NURTURING STRATEGIES:

1. After waking from a nap, promptly remove the infant from the crib.
2. Talking about the nap will provide the infant with information about his behavior. Comments might include:

   "Lakota, you must be so rested. You slept a long time."
3. Begin to investigate whether other basic needs require your attention. For example, check to see if the infant is wet or hungry. Comments to make include:

   "Lakota, let's check your diaper. You might be wet after that long nap."

   "Are you hungry? It's been a long time since you ate."
4. Respond to the vocalizations of the infant with conversation. To illustrate, comment:

   "Lakota, you are wet. I'll change you."

☼ Highlighting Development

After birth, infants may sleep 16 or more hours per day. Gradually, their need for sleep decreases, while the need for stimulation increases.

VARIATION:

♡ Repeat this activity during eating. Always hold the infant while feeding and look into his eyes. Be warm and loving. Smile, coo, and talk to the child.

ADDITIONAL INFORMATION:

♡ Promptly meeting infants' basic needs fosters a sense of trust. They quickly learn they can depend on you for help during periods of discomfort or distress.

DEVELOPMENTAL AREA: **Social**

I'll Help

SOCIAL

Child's Developmental Goals

✓ To develop a sense of trust

✓ To experience social interactions

MATERIALS:

None

PREPARATION:

♡ Observe the infant's signals for signs of readiness.

NURTURING STRATEGIES:

1. When an infant signals you, move to the child's side immediately while verbally describing what you can see or hear. Say, for example:
   "Midori is crying. She sounds very upset. I'm coming, Midori. I'm here to help."
2. Using your knowledge of the infant, provide comfort.
3. Use your voice as a tool to communicate calmness and reassurance.
4. Verbally describe what you are doing for the infant while you are performing the action. For example, state:
   "I'm wrapping you tightly in a blanket. Midori, you like to be warm."

5. Continue the social interaction once the child is calm if the infant signals she wants to interact by smiling or gazing at you.

☼ Highlighting Development

The relationship between infants and adults is believed to be the foundation for later relationships with adults and peers. If infants learn to trust adults, they tend to have more positive relationships with peers later in life (Cassidy, Scolton, Kirsh, & Parke, 1996; Park & Waters, 1989).

VARIATION:

♡ Try other techniques for soothing a crying infant described in the Introduction (see pp. 10–11).

ADDITIONAL INFORMATION:

♡ Paying close attention to an infant's signals is vital for developing a positive relationship. Infants need to know that you can be counted on to meet their needs.

Emotional Development

BIRTH to THREE MONTHS

DEVELOPMENTAL AREA: **Emotional**

Labeling Emotions

EMOTIONAL

Child's Developmental Goals

✓ To express the basic emotions of distress, disgust, and interest

✓ To learn self-soothing techniques

MATERIALS:

None

PREPARATION:

♡ Constantly observe the infant. When an infant is displaying an emotion such as distress, disgust, or interest, respond immediately.

NURTURING STRATEGIES:

1. Using your observation skills and knowledge of the situation, describe and label the infant's emotions. Comments include:
   "Tunde, you are crying. You must be hungry. You need to eat. Let's warm a bottle. It is hard to wait."
   "You are angry. You don't enjoy having your diaper changed. We're almost done. I'm pulling up your pants."
2. Assist the infant in developing self-soothing techniques. For example, providing a pacifier or rattle to suck on can sooth a distressed infant.
3. Describe how the self-soothing technique was beneficial to the infant. Say, for example:
   "The rattle is helping. You are calming down."

☀ Highlighting Development

During the first few months, babies appear to cry more frequently as a means of communication. They may cry for many reasons other than anger, sadness, or fear. They also cry because they are hungry, cold, or have a wet diaper. Moreover, they may also cry if they want company because they are lonely or bored.

VARIATION:

♡ Try using other techniques for reducing stress: changing the diaper, feeding, holding, moving to a new position, covering with a blanket, etc.

ADDITIONAL INFORMATION:

♡ For infants, crying is a way of communicating. Therefore, infants cry for a variety of reasons, including anger, sadness, or fear. Careful observation of infants is necessary to accurately label their emotions and needs.

♡ Each infant has a unique emotion rhythm. Observe carefully and make mental notes. Then respond accordingly.

Finding Your Fist

Child's Developmental Goals

✓ To recognize basic emotions—distress, disgust, and interest

✓ To learn self-soothing techniques

MATERIALS:

None

PREPARATION:

None

NURTURING STRATEGIES:

1. During nap time when the infant is fussy, provide verbal encouragement for sucking on a fist. Say, for example:
   "Tara, you are fussy. Sucking on your fist may help."
   "Put your fist in your mouth."
2. If more than verbal encouragement is needed, physically guide the infant's fist to the mouth. Encourage the infant to suck the fist. Make comments such as:
   "Tara, that's better. You are soothing yourself."
3. Speaking in a quiet, soft voice also assists in soothing the infant.

 ## Highlighting Development

Infants crave tactile stimulation, which plays an important part in their emotional development. Through tactile stimulation from being held and caressed by their caregivers, infants develop attachment behaviors. When they have healthy interactions with nurturing caregivers, infants become better prepared to learn from and deal with the stressors of everyday life (Shore, 1997).

VARIATION:

♡ Sucking on a pacifier or infant toy can also be self-soothing.

ADDITIONAL INFORMATION:

♡ Infants enjoy sucking for its sheer pleasure. Fists are preferable over pacifiers because the infant is in control. The tool is immediately available. Moreover, teaching infants to suck on their fists should not promote thumb sucking.

 Exercise caution and sanitize toys before giving them to an infant. A bleach solution to sanitize an infant's toys can be prepared by mixing 1 tablespoon of household bleach with 1 gallon of water. After immersing the toys in the bleach solution, let them air dry.

DEVELOPMENTAL AREA: **Emotional**

"Hickory, Dickory, Dock"

Child's Developmental Goals

✓ To express basic emotions—distress, disgust, enjoyment, and interest

✓ To respond to the emotional expressions of others

✓ To practice responding with a smile during social interactions

MATERIALS:

None

PREPARATION:

♡ Observe the child's state of alertness to determine when the rhyme should be introduced. If the infant is sleepy, delay this activity.

NURTURING STRATEGIES:

1. After diapering the child and before removing the child from the changing table, chant the nursery rhyme "Hickory, Dickory, Dock."

2. While chanting the nursery rhyme, walk your fingers up and down the infant's body.

3. During this interaction, respond to the infant's display of emotions by labeling his feelings. Make comments such as:
   "Umberto, you are laughing. What a happy baby."
   "What a big smile. Umberto, does this tickle?"

4. During this interaction, smile. Because infants imitate, your expression should elicit a smile.

5. Continue chanting the nursery rhyme as long as the infant appears interested. Check to see that the child is maintaining eye contact or smiling.

☀ Highlighting Development

An emotion is a feeling that motivates, organizes, and guides perception, thought, and action (Izard, 1991). For healthy well–being, the emotional expression of all feelings is important to develop. Therefore, infants need to learn self-soothing techniques for coping with sadness, anger, or frustration. Coping with these emotions is more difficult than coping with happiness.

VARIATIONS:

♡ While singing a song about emotions, move the infant to the rhythm.

♡ Finger plays may be substituted for songs. See Appendix F for a list of finger plays to use with infants.

ADDITIONAL INFORMATION:

♡ Infants will learn appropriate emotional expression and regulation through close, sensitive contact with adults.

♡ In the beginning, emotional reactions for the infant are involuntary and cannot be controlled.

EMOTIONAL

Who's That in the Mirror?

Child's Developmental Goals

✓ To show different emotions, such as enjoyment, interest, or disgust

✓ To regulate self-expression of emotions

MATERIALS:

❑ Blanket or mat
❑ Nonbreakable mirror

PREPARATION:

♡ Select an area that can be constantly supervised. Clear a space for the mirror and blanket or mat.

NURTURING STRATEGIES:

1. Lay the infant facedown on the blanket or mat.
2. Tapping lightly on the mirror typically gains the infant's attention. If the infant looks into the mirror, say, for example:
   "Who's that in the mirror? There is Christina."
   If the infant doesn't look into the mirror, providing more verbal cues may be necessary. Comments include:
   "Christina, push yourself up."
   "Raise up your head."
   "Look here, there's a baby."
   You may also try moving the mirror to attract the infant's attention.
3. While the infant is looking in the mirror, describe your observations, focusing on emotions. For example, remark:
   "Christina, you are smiling. What a happy baby."
   "You raised your head. You must be proud."

4. Provide positive reinforcement or encouragement as needed. Statements such as the following could be made:
   "Christina, it is hard to keep your head raised."
   "You are working hard."

☀ Highlighting Development

Infants show facial expressions that appear to convey their emotional states. They smile when they appear happy. They show anger when frustrated. When they are unhappy, they look sad (Feldman, 1998). Respond to children's cues and clues. Their rhythms and moods are evident even during the first days and weeks of life. Respond to them when they are upset, as well as when they are happy. Try to understand what children are feeling, what they are communicating to you, and what they are trying to do (Shore, 1997).

VARIATION:

♡ Holding a small mirror while the infant is sitting in your lap will reduce the physical exertion of this activity for the infant, yet still provide an outlet for emotional talk.

ADDITIONAL INFORMATION:

♡ Surrounding the infant with "emotional talk" will assist her in learning how to recognize and label emotions. These are very important skills for young children to develop.

🚸 Whenever pillows or blankets are used, constant supervision is necessary to prevent the possibility of suffocation.

DEVELOPMENTAL AREA: **Emotional**

Resting with Lullabies

EMOTIONAL

Child's Developmental Goals

✓ To relax by listening to music

✓ To develop self-soothing skills

MATERIALS:

☐ Crib

☐ Tape or compact disc of lullabies

☐ Tape or compact disc player

PREPARATION:

♡ Select a lullaby, place the tape or compact disc in the player, and set the player in a safe place.

NURTURING STRATEGIES:

1. Lay the infant faceup in the crib.
2. Rubbing the infant's abdomen using soft, gentle strokes while humming or singing to the music will help the child relax.
3. With music playing in the background, comment:
   "What soft music. It helps you calm down."
   "This music makes you sleepy."
   "Listen to the music."
4. Walking away before the infant falls asleep will support the development of self-regulation skills by providing the opportunity to finish calming down.

 Highlighting Development

During this stage, infants express emotions not only through facial expressions or vocalizations but also with their entire bodies. For example, when interested in objects, infants may gaze at them while moving their arms and legs in anticipation.

VARIATION:

♡ By using different types of music such as nature tapes or classical music, the development of appreciation for a wide variety of sounds and sound patterns will be fostered.

ADDITIONAL INFORMATION:

♡ The role of the caregiver cannot be overemphasized for this activity. For this experience to be effective, the caregiver must be calm and soothing. Consequently, rushing while rubbing the infant's abdomen may cause the infant to be overstimulated rather than relaxed.

 Given the threat of Sudden Infant Death Syndrome, always lay infants faceup in cribs.

Friends Have Feelings Too

Child's Developmental Goals

✓ To identify the emotions of interest, enjoyment, disgust, and distress

✓ To become aware that other people have emotions

Highlighting Development

By three months, infants show interest in sounds by turning their heads toward the source. When this happens, explaining the sound is imperative to their cognitive, language, and emotional development.

MATERIALS:

None

PREPARATION:

♡ Observe the infant for a "teachable moment." Watch to see what is captivating the child, then interact.

NURTURING STRATEGIES:

1. When an infant turns toward another person who is displaying an emotion, reinforce this behavior by discussing feelings. Comment by saying:
"You are looking at Zach. He is sad. He is crying. Zach wants his mommy."
"You are watching Simone. She is laughing. She is exploring the rattle. Listen to Simone shake it."

2. Continue the conversation by connecting an emotional display of the other person to the life experiences of the infant to whom you are talking. To illustrate, you might say:
"When you are hungry, you sometimes cry."
"You like rattles. They are fun to shake."

VARIATION:

♡ Using emotional talk, speak to infants by describing their emotional expressions.

ADDITIONAL INFORMATION:

♡ Infants are interested in an assortment of sounds, especially those made by humans. Therefore, it is important to introduce them to a variety of sounds.

♡ Observe. Most infants will begin to coo between five and eight weeks of age. Cooing can be interpreted as an expression of comfort, enjoyment, satisfaction, or interest.

"This Little Piggy"

Child's Developmental Goals

✓ To share the emotions of interest and enjoyment

✓ To respond to the emotional expressions of others

MATERIALS:

None

PREPARATION:

♡ Observe the infant's signal for interaction.

NURTURING STRATEGIES:

1. If the infant's toes are exposed during the diaper-changing procedure, recite the nursery rhyme "This Little Piggy." If the infant's toes are covered, remove clothing to expose the toes.
2. While reciting the nursery rhyme, lightly shake the infant's toes.
3. Look into the baby's face and respond to his expression. Your expressions will provide cues to the infant as to how to respond. Therefore, while lightly shaking the infant's toes, you should share a smile.
4. Describing the infant's reactions to this game will provide meaningful information about emotional content and expression. Comments might include: *"Look at that smile. Hemant, you like this game." "Hemant, now you are laughing."*
5. Observing the infant's cues will allow you to stop this game before it becomes overwhelming. When the infant is frowning or avoiding eye contact, it is time to end the interaction.

Highlighting Development

Infants actively participate in their own brain development by signaling their needs to caregivers and by responding selectively to different kinds of stimulation (Shore, 1997). For example, when children become bored, they may cry to elicit being picked up and moved to another location.

VARIATION:

♡ Recite a different nursery rhyme that also encourages touching. See Appendix F for a list of nursery rhymes.

ADDITIONAL INFORMATION:

♡ Caregivers must observe and monitor the level of infant stimulation. Even though infants can signal overstimulation, they are unable to completely remove themselves from the situation because of their lack of mobility. Therefore, you must pay close attention and quickly respond to the body and vocal signals given by infants.

♡ Observe. The infant will respond to the drama of your body language such as the brightening of your eyes and playfulness of your voice.

Physical Development

FOUR to SIX MONTHS

Fluttering Tree

PHYSICAL

Child's Developmental Goals

✓ To refine eye-hand coordination skills

✓ To practice reaching and strengthening arm muscles

MATERIALS:

❑ Wool yarn cut in an 18-inch section for each toy

❑ 2 or 3 interesting infant toys

PREPARATION:

♡ Attach one end of the yarn to each of the toys. Then tie the other end of the yarn around the structure allowing the toy to hang. Adjust the yarn so that the infant can easily reach the toys while being held.

NURTURING STRATEGIES:

1. Carry the infant over to the suspended toys.
2. Touch the toys with your hands and describe what is happening. Comment by saying:
   "Antonia, I touched the toys. Watch me. I used my hand."
3. Invite the infant to touch the toys using the hands by saying:
   "Can you touch the toys? Grab them. Use your hands."
4. Raise the infant up so that the toys will easily move with a swipe of a hand.
5. Praise the infant for touching/moving the toys. Examples might include saying:
   "Antonia, you did it. You moved the toys!"
6. Position the infant so that the toys are a little farther away. Then invite the infant to move the toys again.
7. Encourage the infant to try by saying:
   "Reach, Antonia, reach. You can do it! Grab the toy."
   If the toys move or are caught, praise the infant's accomplishment. If the infant misses, provide further encouragement.
8. If the infant swipes but continues to miss, move him closer to the toys so that he experiences success.

☀ Highlighting Development

Hand-eye coordination is improving. At three months of age, the infant is swiping at objects in an uncoordinated fashion. Among the movement milestones accomplished during this stage, the infant will reach with one hand to obtain desired objects. Using a raking motion, she will be able to pick up the objects.

By six months of age, most infants have a sophisticated way of reaching for and grasping objects. They can focus on an object at a distance and direct their hands straight to it. Moreover, they can adjust their hand to fit the size of the object they are grasping. At this time, they may manipulate, bang, or bring the objects to their mouths in a coordinated manner (Bentzen, 2001).

VARIATION:

♡ Use a longer string so that the infant can reach for the toys while lying on a blanket.

ADDITIONAL INFORMATION:

♡ Observe how young children love to pull on yarn strings. Repeated practice in pulling the strings will help teach them problem-solving skills in obtaining desired objects.

 For safety purposes, use wool yarn because it breaks easily. To prevent strangulation, constant supervision is always necessary when using yarn. Toys with cords, ribbons, string, rope, or ties should be avoided with young children. They could become wrapped around the infant's neck or wrists.

PHYSICAL

Rolling Over

Child's Developmental Goals

✓ To practice rolling from side to back
✓ To practice visually tracking an object

MATERIALS:

❑ 1 or 2 interesting infant toys
❑ Blanket or mat

PREPARATION:

♡ Select an area that can be constantly supervised. Clear this area and spread out the blanket or mat.

NURTURING STRATEGIES:

1. Lay the infant on a side on the blanket.
2. Gain the infant's attention by showing and describing the toys one at a time. Comment by saying:
   "Nikko, this is an elephant. It has a long nose."
3. Move the toys out of the infant's line of sight. Encourage the infant to search for the toys. Say, for example:
   "Where did the elephant go? Look for it. Roll over."
4. If the infant rolls or attempts to do so, provide positive reinforcement. To illustrate, say:
   "Nikko, you are working hard."
   "You rolled over!"
5. If the infant does not visually search for the toy, move the toy back into the infant's line of vision. Slowly move the toy while the infant tracks it visually. Continue to move the toy until the infant rolls from the side to back. Provide encouragement and reinforcement as needed.

 Highlighting Development

An infant's vision is improving at this stage of development. Everything he does he watches closely. Vision now is playing an important role in his physical development. Color recognition skills are emerging. Chances are the infant will recognize blue, green, red, and yellow compared to other colors (Berk, 1997).

VARIATIONS:

♡ When developmentally ready, begin to practice rolling from back to side.
♡ Use soft, textured balls that make pleasant sounds when moved.

ADDITIONAL INFORMATION:

♡ Hiding toys on both the left and right sides of the infant's body will promote the uniform development of the child's muscles.

CAUTION Consider safety precautions when selecting toys for infants. Beware of toys containing removable small parts. If removed, these can become lodged in nostrils, ears, or windpipes.

CAUTION Always check mouthable toys for safety. Make sure they are at least two inches in diameter. Use the core of a toilet paper roll to measure; if a toy can fit inside the cardboard core, it is too small for an infant.

CAUTION Whenever pillows or blankets are used, constant supervision is necessary to prevent the possibility of suffocation.

All Propped Up!

PHYSICAL

4 to 6 months

Child's Developmental Goals

✓ To strengthen lower back muscles

✓ To sit in an upright "tripod" position with assistance

MATERIALS:

❑ Blanket or mat
❑ Pillows or rolled quilt
❑ Toy

PREPARATION:

♡ Observe the infant. Once she is strong enough to raise her chest off the floor when in a facedown position, you can help her practice sitting up.

♡ Select an area that you can constantly supervise. Clear this area and spread out the blanket or mat.

♡ Lay out the pillows or rolled quilt on the blanket for support and a safe fall zone.

NURTURING STRATEGIES:

1. Sit the infant upright on the blanket. To assist the infant in balancing, spread the legs apart to create a wide base. If necessary, rearrange the pillows or rolled quilt so the infant is securely supported.

2. Once the infant is steady and sitting without your assistance, provide positive reinforcement. Make comments such as:
   "Look at Imani. You are sitting up."
   "What a strong baby!"

3. Encourage the infant to visually explore the room. Say, for example:
   "Look around, Imani. What can you see?"
   "Look at the toy clown."

4. Constant supervision is always necessary to protect the child from bodily harm and suffocation.

☀ Highlighting Development

When infants are able to raise their chest from the floor, they are ready to begin sitting with assistance. Although infants desire to sit, they are unable to do this alone. They need help getting into the sitting position and balancing once there.

VARIATION:

♡ Provide a toy for the infant to explore with both hands and mouth while sitting up. Note that the infant may attempt to transfer items from one hand to the other.

 Constant supervision is necessary.

 Infants often topple over while learning to sit. To promote their safety, create a fall zone by surrounding them with cushioning materials, such as pillows or blankets.

Whenever pillows or blankets are used, constant supervision is necessary to prevent the possibility of suffocation.

PHYSICAL

Holding On

Child's Developmental Goals

✓ To practice the ulnar grasp

✓ To develop the lower back muscles

✓ To practice transferring objects from one hand to the other

MATERIALS:

❑ Cube at least 3 inches in diameter

❑ Blanket or mat

❑ Pillows or rolled quilt

PREPARATION:

♡ Select an area that you can constantly supervise. Clear this area and spread out the blanket or mat.

♡ Because most infants this age will be unable to sit without assistance, lay out the pillows or the rolled quilt on the blanket for support and to create a fall zone.

NURTURING STRATEGIES:

1. Sit the infant upright on the blanket. To help promote balance, spread the infant's legs in a tripod position to create a wide base of support.

2. Once the infant is steady, offer the cube while talking about it. Comments might include:
   "Forrest, look. Here is a cube. It is red. The cube is smooth."

3. Encourage the infant to explore the cube with both hands and mouth. Foster these skills by saying:
   "Forrest, touch it with your other hand."
   "Put it in your left hand."

☀ Highlighting Development

When the reflexive grasp of the newborn weakens, it is replaced by the ulnar grasp, a clumsy motion in which the fingers close against the palm (Berk, 1997). Objects are held by all four fingers, which is why it is sometimes referred to as the mitten grasp. Eventually, objects will be held by only one or two fingers against the palm.

VARIATION:

♡ Provide other stimulating toys for the infant to observe, hold, or explore in a sitting position.

ADDITIONAL INFORMATION:

♡ Labeling the hands left and right serves only to alert the infant that there are two hands and they are slightly different. Infants will be unable to accurately demonstrate understanding of which hand is the right one and which hand is the left one.

♡ Select toys carefully to avoid safety hazards and promote development. See Appendix B for a list of criteria to aid in your selection.

 Whenever pillows or blankets are used, constant supervision is necessary to prevent the possibility of suffocation.

Activity Gym

Child's Developmental Goals

✓ To develop eye-hand coordination skills

✓ To practice using the ulnar grasp

MATERIALS:

❑ Blanket

❑ Activity gym

PREPARATION:

♡ Select an area that can be constantly supervised. Clear this area and spread out the blanket.

♡ Place the activity gym on the blanket.

NURTURING STRATEGIES:

1. Lay the infant faceup on the blanket under the activity gym.

2. Gain the infant's attention by shaking the toys hanging from the activity gym. Describe the objects while touching them. Comment, for example:

   "Darcy, look at the black bear. It makes a noise."

3. Encourage the infant to reach for or grab the toys by saying:

   "Darcy, reach. Stretch. Touch the bear."
   "You touched it! Now grab it."

4. Reinforce the infant's attempts and accomplishments. To illustrate, state:

   "You grabbed the bear. It is soft."
   "Darcy, you are shaking the toy. You are working hard."

☀ Highlighting Development

After infants are able to bring objects to their mouth, they will begin using their fingers and palm in a raking motion. This type of hand development can be stimulated by placing objects within reach. Furthermore, infants are learning the importance of using their hands.

VARIATION:

♡ Make your own activity gym by suspending toys with wool yarn from a table.

ADDITIONAL INFORMATION:

♡ Infants need responsive toys to learn about cause and effect. They need toys to bat, hit, bang, and shake.

Be proactive by checking the stability of the activity gym. If the activity gym is on an uneven surface, it might not be able to support the child's weight and, therefore, it could be a risk to the child's safety.

Carefully observe the infant working with the activity gym. Make sure the infant's body is not pulled off the ground or floor.

Suspended toys can become dangerous if used too long. Once infants begin sitting or getting on their hands or knees, these toys should be removed (Abrams & Kaufman, 1990).

Whenever pillows or blankets are used, constant supervision is necessary to prevent the possibility of suffocation.

Grabbing and Pulling

Child's Developmental Goals

✓ To practice the ulnar grasp

✓ To strengthen the upper and lower arm muscles

MATERIALS:

❏ Blanket or mat

❏ Wooden spool

❏ 12-inch piece of elastic

❏ Diaper pin

❏ Masking tape

PREPARATION:

♡ Prepare this game by securing the wooden spool to the elastic. Attach one end of the elastic around the center of the spool with the diaper pin.

♡ Select an area that you can constantly supervise. Clear this area for the blanket or mat.

NURTURING STRATEGIES:

1. Lay the infant faceup on the blanket.
2. Gain the infant's attention by lowering the spool into the child's line of vision, pointing to the spool, and saying:
   "Parker, look at this spool. Grab it."
3. Reinforce any attempts to grab the spool by commenting:
   "You touched it. Now grab it."
   "You are holding the spool, Parker."
4. When the infant has grasped the spool, say:
   "Hold on tight. I'm going to pull the spool."
   While saying this, begin gently tugging on the elastic.

5. Encourage the infant to exercise arm muscles by explaining:
   "Now, you pull it, Parker."
   "Pull. You are pulling the spool."
6. Providing positive reinforcement may help to sustain the interaction. Comments might include:
   "What a strong baby."
   "Keep pulling. Wow, you have strong arms."

☀ Highlighting Development

Infants' hands are becoming more functional now. As their hand–eye coordination improves, they will begin grabbing their feet and bringing them to their mouth. They may also clap their hands against the thighs. Through these physical activities, they are also discovering new sensorimotor sensations.

VARIATION:

♡ Attach any favorite toy to the piece of elastic.

ADDITIONAL INFORMATION:

♡ The strength of the infant may surprise you. Keeping a tight grasp on the elastic will prevent the infant from being injured by the spool. If the elastic snaps, the child could be hit by the spool.

 After closing diaper pins, always secure them by wrapping with masking tape.

 Whenever pillows or blankets are used, constant supervision is necessary to prevent the possibility of suffocation.

Pulling Up to Sit

PHYSICAL

Child's Developmental Goals

✓ To strengthen the lower back muscles

✓ To gain balance in a sitting position

MATERIALS:

❑ Blanket or mat

PREPARATION:

♡ Select an area that can be constantly supervised. Clear the area and spread out the blanket or mat.

NURTURING STRATEGIES:

1. Lay the infant faceup on the blanket.
2. Talk to the infant about what is going to happen by commenting:
   "Amanda, give me your hands. Hold them out."
   "I'm going to help you sit up."
3. Reinforcing your words with actions may be necessary. If this is the case, repeat the words:
   "Give me your hands."
   While speaking, take the infant's hands.
4. Gently pull the infant into a sitting position. If necessary, spread the infant's legs in a tripod position to create a wide base of support.
5. Continue to support the infant in the sitting position.

6. Provide positive reinforcement so that the infant begins to understand what is happening. Say, for example:
   "Amanda, you pulled yourself up. You are sitting now."
   "What a strong baby. You can sit up."

☼ Highlighting Development

By leaning forward and extending their arms in a tripod position, infants learn to balance their upper bodies. This position is used to avoid falling when attempting to sit up. Eventually, infants will be able to sit using just their legs to support their body weight.

VARIATION:

♡ Whenever the child is lying flat and needs to be picked up, help the infant move into a sitting position first.

ADDITIONAL INFORMATION:

♡ Often infants enjoy repetition; therefore, repeat the activity until the infant signals a lack of interest.

⊘ CAUTION Whenever pillows or blankets are used, constant supervision is necessary to prevent the possibility of suffocation.

4 to 6 months

Language and Communication Development

FOUR to SIX MONTHS

"Pat-A-Cake"

Child's Developmental Goals

✓ To hear native language patterns

✓ To associate words with actions

MATERIALS:

❏ Blanket or mat

PREPARATION:

♡ Select an area that can be constantly supervised. Clear this area and spread out the blanket or mat.

NURTURING STRATEGIES:

1. Lay the infant faceup on a blanket or mat.
2. Gain the infant's attention by chanting (clap to rhythm) "Pat-A-Cake" while performing the actions:

Pat-a-cake, pat-a-cake	(clap to the rhythm)
Baker's man.	(clap to the rhythm)
Bake me a cake	(clap to the rhythm)
As fast as you can.	(clap to the rhythm)
Roll it	(roll hands)
And pat it	(pat belly)
And mark it with a *J*	(insert first letter of child's name)
And put it in the oven	
For *Jamal* and me	(point to infant and then self)

3. Stimulate the infant by talking about reactions to the song. For example, say:
   "*Jamal, you are smiling. Did you like it when I patted your belly?*"

4. Repeat the song as long as the infant shows interest. Signs of interest include smiling, cooing, and maintaining eye contact.

☼ Highlighting Development

Because of increased control over their vocal mechanisms, infants begin to babble during this stage, typically between 6 and 10 months of age. Listen carefully to them. You should hear infants beginning to combine consonants and vowels in alternating sequences heard in their native language. While cooing focused on vowels, babbling shifts toward a focus on consonants. Typical combinations include "ma ma ma," "da da da," and "ba ba ba" (Snow, 1998).

VARIATION:

♡ Hold the infant in a position that allows you to visually connect while reciting the chant.

ADDITIONAL INFORMATION:

♡ Infants need to engage in one-on-one, face-to-face interactions with adults. During this time, they learn trust, security, and language skills.

♡ Repeat any recognizable sounds the infant makes by parroting them.

 Whenever pillows or blankets are used, constant supervision is necessary to prevent the possibility of suffocation.

Babble Time

Child's Developmental Goals

✓ To practice producing babbling sounds

✓ To develop language skills

MATERIALS:

None

PREPARATION:

♡ Observe the infant. Is the child babbling spontaneously? Does the child appear to be seeking social interaction? For example, is the infant looking around the room or gazing toward you?

NURTURING STRATEGIES:

1. If the infant appears to want interaction, move closer to the infant. Position yourself so that you can visually connect with the infant. If desired, hold the child.

2. Listen to the vocalizations made by the infant. When the infant pauses, imitate the child's vocalizations. Pause. Your pausing will encourage the infant to vocalize again.

3. To add a twist to the conversation, create a new string of babble during your turn. Observe closely to see if the infant imitates your vocalizations.

4. Providing positive reinforcement may encourage the infant to continue babbling. For example, say:
   "Mahala, we are talking."
   "You are talking a lot today, Mahala. Tell me more."

☀ Highlighting Development

Talkativeness by young children partly depends on the stimulation they receive from adults around them. Therefore, you need to frequently talk and converse with infants (Leach, 1992).

Infants respond to sounds by making sounds. The ease, fluency, and complexity with which infants babble is closely related to the ease and speed with which they will later learn to use expressive language.

Note that before they can see differences between facial expressions, infants can detect different emotions in the voice. By five months of age, infants will listen longer to a voice expressing approval than one expressing disapproval (Fogel, 2001).

VARIATIONS:

♡ When a recognizable sound is made, parrot it back to the infant.

♡ Introduce new syllables.

ADDITIONAL INFORMATION:

♡ Many infants engage in private "conversations" as a way of improving their language skills. Therefore, infants also need time to practice babbling in private.

♡ Listen to the infant voice for signs of pleasure and displeasure. This will be a clue to continue or discontinue the activity.

4 to 6 months

What's Coming Up?

Child's Developmental Goals

✓ To develop receptive language skills

✓ To hear native language patterns

MATERIALS:

None

PREPARATION:

♡ Observe the infant's level of alertness to determine the appropriate time to introduce the experience.

NURTURING STRATEGIES:

1. This activity can be introduced any time you are transitioning the child from one activity or routine to another. Prepare the infant for the upcoming event by verbally describing it.

2. Let the infant know what the transition will include. Examples of comments include:
    "After I wash your hands, we can go for a stroller ride. You like being outside."
    "After I wash your hands, I will lay you in your crib. You are so sleepy. Would you like to hear a song?"
    "Before you eat, your hands need to be washed."
    "I'll read you a book before you take your nap."

☀ Highlighting Development

Routines create an environment of predictability and consistency for infants by providing a pattern. Preparing the infant for the next step in the routine is necessary to foster a sense of security.

VARIATION:

♡ Infants also enjoy songs. Therefore, to add variety try communicating the change of routines by singing. (For a variety of finger plays and songs, see Appendix D and Appendix E, respectively.)

ADDITIONAL INFORMATION:

♡ Discussing what will happen creates a context for future events and promotes the development of auditory memory skills.

"Bumping Up and Down"

Child's Developmental Goals

✓ To associate words with actions

✓ To develop receptive language skills

MATERIALS:

❑ Song, "Bumping Up and Down"

❑ Tagboard or index card and felt–tip marker

PREPARATION:

♡ If you have memorized the words to the song "Bumping Up and Down," no preparation is needed. However, if you need a prompt, create a poster or note card with the words and actions.

NURTURING STRATEGIES:

1. In a sitting position, hold the infant on your knees so that you can visually connect and gently bounce.
2. Sing the following song:

   ♫ Bumping up and down in a little red wagon (bounce child on knee)

   ♫ Bumping up and down in a little red wagon (bounce child on knee)

   ♫ Bumping up and down in a little red wagon (bounce child on knee)

   ♫ Won't you be my darling?

   ♫ One wheel's gone and the axle's broken (bounce child on knee)

   ♫ One wheel's gone and the axle's broken (bounce child on knee)

   ♫ One wheel's gone and the axle's broken (bounce child on knee)

   ♫ Won't you be my darling?

   ♫ Josiah gonna fix it with his hammer (make motion of tool)

   ♫ Josiah gonna fix it with his hammer (make motion of tool)

   ♫ Josiah gonna fix it with his hammer (make motion of tool)

   ♫ Won't you be my darling?

3. Substitute different people such as a parent, sibling, or friend in the song. Tools such as hammers, pliers, and rulers can also be substituted in subsequent verses.
4. Continue singing this song as long as the infant shows interest by maintaining eye contact and smiling.

☀ Highlighting Development

Children learn the sounds of their native language through repeated exposure. During this stage, the children's babbling imitates the rhythm and sounds they have been exposed to. Listen carefully. You will observe that infants drop their voice as when making a statement. They also raise their voice as when asking a question.

VARIATION:

♡ Recite a nursery rhyme while performing accompanying actions.

ADDITIONAL INFORMATION:

♡ This is a very long song. You may want to sing only the first verse, pause, and then sing the second verse if the child is interested.

Telling Picture Book Stories

4 to 6 months

Child's Developmental Goals

✔ To develop receptive language skills

✔ To produce babbling sounds

MATERIALS:

❑ Picture book

PREPARATION:

♡ Observe the child's state of alertness to determine the most appropriate timing of the experience.

♡ Place the book in an accessible location.

NURTURING STRATEGIES:

1. Hold the infant in your lap so that both of you can view the book.
2. Gain the infant's attention by saying:
   "Esme, I have a book. It is about kittens. You like kittens. Let's look at it together."
3. Begin "reading" the book. Describe the pictures while pointing to them.
4. Engage the infant in conversation by pointing to the picture and asking questions such as:
   "Esme, what is this kitten doing?"
   "What is this?"
5. Pause to allow the infant the opportunity to respond by babbling.
6. Reinforce the infant's response through comments like:
   "That's right, Esme. The kitten is pushing a ball."
7. If the infant maintains interest through such actions as smiling and babbling, consider reading the book again.

 ## Highlighting Development

Infants learn turn-taking skills when adults model this behavior. To illustrate, adults first should ask a question. Then they need to pause, allowing the infant an opportunity to respond by babbling. After the infant produces a recognizable syllable, it needs to be responded to or echoed back.

VARIATION:

♡ Prepare a picture book based upon the infant's interests. Pictures can be obtained through magazines or actual photographs of the child, family, and the immediate environment.

ADDITIONAL INFORMATION:

♡ Choose picture books that are sturdy and have one large picture per page. Preferably, the pictures should reflect items in the child's immediate environment. At this stage of development, infants are unable to follow story lines, making print unnecessary.

♡ Cardboard picture books are easier for you and the infant to handle. In addition, these books are more durable.

"One, Two, Buckle . . ."

Child's Developmental Goals

✓ To hear native language patterns
✓ To develop rhythm

MATERIALS:

❑ Infant seat
❑ Index card and felt-tip marker

PREPARATION:

♡ If needed, write out the words to the nursery rhyme "One, Two, Buckle My Shoe" on an index card. Carry this in your pocket for quick reference.
♡ Select and clear an area to place the infant seat.

NURTURING STRATEGIES:

1. Secure the infant in the seat using the safety restraint.
2. Position your body so that you can visually connect with the infant and any other children in your care.
3. Gain the infant's attention by reciting the following nursery rhyme:

   One, two, buckle my shoe
   Three, four, shut the door
   Five, six, pick up sticks
   Seven, eight, lay them straight
   Nine, ten a big tall hen.

4. While reciting the nursery rhyme, lightly tap the infant's leg with your hand to the rhythm of the rhyme.
5. Continue reciting this nursery rhyme as long as the infant shows interest through vocalizing, smiling, making body movements, or maintaining eye contact.

☀ Highlighting Development

An infant's first exposure to rhythm is through listening to his mother's heartbeat while in the womb. Rhythms such as a whirling fan or ticking clock help an infant to block external or internal discomforts. Thus, communication through rhythms plays an important part in the infant's development.

VARIATION:

♡ Sing songs or do finger plays that have steady, easy rhythms. See Appendix D for finger plays and Appendix E for songs.

ADDITIONAL INFORMATION:

♡ At this stage of development, counting is used to develop rhythm rather than for promoting the understanding of numerical concepts.

Conversing

Child's Developmental Goals

✓ To practice turn-taking skills

✓ To develop expressive language skills

MATERIALS:

None

PREPARATION:

♡ Gathering all diapering supplies may facilitate the activity and allow you to focus on the child.

NURTURING STRATEGIES:

1. While diapering the child, talk about what you are doing. Comments include:
   "Anika, I'm putting on my gloves. They keep me safe."
   "This might be cold. I'm going to clean your bottom with the wipe."
2. Engage the infant in conversation by asking questions such as:
   "What happens next?"
3. Pause to provide the infant time to respond by babbling.
4. Reinforce the infant's response. Use comments such as:
   "Anika, yes. I need to sanitize the table."
   "Well, I need to put on the clean diaper first."

☀ Highlighting Development

Modeling language plays an important role in the child's development. Only through exposure do infants learn to make more complicated sounds. Consequently, an environment rich in language usually results in the infant generating more speech.

VARIATIONS:

♡ Talk about what the infant is looking at.
♡ Repeat this activity during other routine care times such as feeding.

ADDITIONAL INFORMATION:

♡ Infants learn important language and communication skills while conversing with adults. Therefore, repeating this activity frequently will promote this area of development.

♡ There is similarity in the babbling of infants from all language backgrounds. Even deaf children babble. Because they lack auditory feedback, their babbling tends to stop earlier (Snow, 1998).

♡ If an infant does not respond by babbling at this stage, the child may be having difficulty hearing. A child with frequent ear infections may often experience difficulty hearing. If this occurs, it is advisable to seek medical attention.

4 to 6 months

Cognitive Development

FOUR to SIX MONTHS

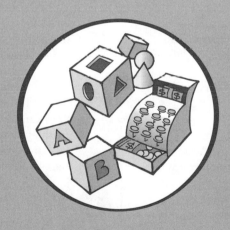

Shaking the Rattle

4 to 6 months

Child's Developmental Goals

✓ To repeatedly engage in purposeful behaviors

✓ To imitate a caregiver's actions

MATERIALS:

❑ 3 rattles of different sizes and sounds

❑ Blanket or mat

PREPARATION:

♡ Select an area that can be constantly supervised. Clear this area and spread out the blanket.

NURTURING STRATEGIES:

1. Lay the infant faceup on a blanket or mat.
2. Gain the infant's attention by shaking and describing the rattles. Make comments such as:
   "Camden, I have three rattles. They all sound different. Listen to them."
3. Lay all three rattles within the infant's reach. Direct the infant to pick one up by saying:
   "Touch a rattle. That's it."
   "Use your hand to pick one up."
4. If necessary, reinforce your words with actions by gently placing the infant's hand on the rattle while repeating:
   "Camden, use your hand to pick one up."
5. Discuss the sound of the chosen rattle. Examples of comments include:
   "That rattle makes a soft sound."
   "That rattle is noisy. It sounds loud."
6. Reinforcing the infant's actions may lead to repetition. Comments include:
   "Shake, shake, shake."
   "Camden, do it again."
   "I want to hear the rattle. Keep shaking."
   "You like shaking the rattle."

☀ Highlighting Development

Infants need to perform actions or behaviors repeatedly in order to add information to their cognitive structures. Therefore, when an infant tires of the activity, stop and repeat it again at a later time.

VARIATIONS:

♡ Supporting the infant in a sitting position gives him a different view while he shakes the rattles.

♡ With the child in a sitting position, repeat the activity using a ball that produces soft music.

ADDITIONAL INFORMATION:

♡ Providing a variety of rattles may gain and sustain the child's interest. See-through rattles that show colors and make noises are particularly attractive.

♡ Change the infant's rattle and toys, allowing the child to have new as well as familiar ones.

 Closely observe infants who are interacting with rattles. To help consumers choose safe toys for children under age three, the U.S. Consumer Product Safety Commission has set part-size standards. The ends of the rattle must be greater than 1⅜ inches in diameter to be safe for infants.

 Appendix B has additional criteria for selecting materials and equipment. Appendix C includes a list of materials and equipment for infants.

 Whenever pillows or blankets are used, constant supervision is necessary to prevent the possibility of suffocation.

Dropping It over the Edge

Child's Developmental Goals

✓ To develop an understanding of object permanence

✓ To develop problem-solving skills

MATERIALS:

❑ High chair

❑ Interesting infant squeeze toys such as a rubber foot

PREPARATION:

♡ Gather the toys and prepare the high chair for the infant.

NURTURING STRATEGIES:

1. Introduce this activity right before lunch when the food or bottle is not quite ready.
2. Securely fasten the infant in the high chair using the safety restraint. Lock the tray in place.
3. Placing the toy foot on the tray may gain the infant's attention. If necessary, comments include:
   "Shannon, look at the toy. Here is the foot. The toes are good for chewing."
4. Observe the infant playing with the toy. Eventually, the infant will drop the toy over the side of the tray. Ask questions to help the infant learn that the object exists even when it can't be seen. For example, ask:
   "Where did the toys go Shannon?"
   "Should we look for the toy?"
5. Provide suggestions of what the infant could do to find the toy. To illustrate, say:
   "Look on the floor."
   "Look around."

6. Reinforce any attempts or accomplishments in looking for the toy by commenting:
   "You are looking for the toy, Shannon!"
7. It may be necessary to reinforce your words with actions. Make comments such as:
   "Here is the toy—it was on the floor," while picking up the toy and handing it back to the infant.

☀ Highlighting Development

Between four and five months, infants refine the principle of cause and effect. By dropping toys on the floor, they learn of their personal ability to influence their environment as they notice a chain of reactions. As a result, they will purposefully continue dropping items.

VARIATIONS:

♡ Repeat this activity, especially steps 4 to 7, any time during the day when a toy has been dropped and forgotten.

♡ Sit the child in an infant seat rather than in a high chair.

ADDITIONAL INFORMATION:

♡ Infants drop objects when the grasping reflex relaxes. At this stage, it is not intentional behavior. This activity helps to teach them to look for the dropped objects.

♡ Use the child's name while engaging in the activity. During this stage, children begin responding to their own names.

Where Is It?

Child's Developmental Goals

✓ To develop an understanding of object permanence

✓ To develop problem-solving skills

MATERIALS:

❑ An interesting infant toy such as a small stuffed animal

❑ Lightweight blanket

PREPARATION:

♡ If available, clear off a child-size table for this activity. Otherwise, a coffee table may be used. Place the stuffed animal on the table.

NURTURING STRATEGIES:

1. Sit down at the table, crossing your legs in a pretzel style. Next, sit the infant in your lap to provide necessary support. Position yourself so that the infant is close to the table.

2. Gain the infant's attention by pointing to, verbally identifying, and describing the toy on the table. To illustrate, say:
   "Tamarron, look at the puppy. It is black and white."
   "See this pig? A pig says 'oink.'"

3. While you have the infant's attention, partially cover the toy with the blanket.

4. Ask the infant:
   "Where did it go? Where is the puppy?"

5. If the infant does not search for the toy, provide hints or suggestions to encourage such behavior:
   "Tamarron, look for the toy."
   "Lift the blanket."

6. Provide positive reinforcement for attempts and accomplishments.
   "Tamarron, you looked. You found the puppy!"
   "You moved the blanket. The pig was hiding!"

☀ Highlighting Development

The infant is now learning a principle called "object permanence." This is the understanding that objects exist even when they are out of view. During this stage, when objects are partially out of sight, the infant typically will search and find the object.

VARIATION:

♡ To increase the difficulty of this activity, partially hide the toy while the infant is attending to other things.

ADDITIONAL INFORMATION:

♡ Encouraging the child to look for the hidden object will assist in the development of an understanding of object permanence.

♡ Infants need different objects with diverse textures (e.g., hard, soft, rough, etc.) They learn through grasping, patting, mouthing, and touching objects. So, give them the toy to explore once the activity is over.

 Whenever pillows or blankets are used, constant supervision is necessary to prevent the possibility of suffocation.

Where Did You Go?

Child's Developmental Goals

✓ To develop an understanding of object permanence

✓ To develop cause-and-effect skills

MATERIALS:

❑ Lightweight blanket
❑ Diapering supplies

PREPARATION:

♡ Gathering all the materials and placing them near the changing table may help facilitate the success of this activity.

NURTURING STRATEGIES:

1. Introduce this activity during and after the diapering routine.
2. Wad the blanket into a small ball and hand it to the infant encouraging her to grasp it with both hands.
3. As the infant raises the blanket to her mouth, the child's face may be blocked from your view. In an excited voice, ask:
   "Where did Stephanie go?"
4. The infant will probably lower her arms to look at you. When this happens, comment:
   "Oh, there you are. Stephanie, you didn't leave!"
5. To foster the development of cause and effect, show interest in the infant's efforts to create movement. For example, say:
   "Stephanie, when you cover your face, I can't see you."

 Highlighting Development

Now infants are more purposeful when engaging with people and items in their immediate environment. Watch. They shake rattles to hear sounds or explore to see what happens. Prior to this stage, infants focus on motor activity while shaking rattles. Now, infants use babbling as a strategy to gain your attention.

VARIATION:

♡ Cover your face with your hands and then ask, *"Where's Stephanie?"*

ADDITIONAL INFORMATION:

♡ Hide-and-seek and peekaboo are favorite games for children from this age to approximately 24 months. Therefore, it is important to repeat these games frequently. Repetition promotes learning and security.

 Whenever pillows or blankets are used, constant supervision is necessary to prevent the possibility of suffocation.

Going Fishing

COGNITIVE

Child's Developmental Goals

✓ To experience the principle of cause and effect

✓ To develop an understanding of object permanence

MATERIALS:

☐ 1 piece of wool yarn
☐ Lightweight toy in the shape of fish

PREPARATION:

♡ Tie one end of the string to the toy fish.

NURTURING STRATEGIES:

1. Sit the infant in a high chair and fasten the safety restraint.
2. While showing the infant the fish, say:
   "Miguel, here is a fish. Look at it. It is on a string."
3. Hanging the fish over the edge of the high chair tray will allow the string to be easily grasped. Encourage the infant to find the fish. Comments include:
   "Find the fish. Where did it go?"
   "Pull the string to find the fish, Miguel."
4. If the infant fails to look for the fish, reinforcing your words with actions may be necessary. To illustrate, while touching the string, say:
   "Pick up the string. Pull it. The fish will come."
5. Providing positive reinforcement may help the infant to continue this game. For example, comment by saying:
   "Miguel, you did it. You pulled the string. The fish came up!"
   "You found the fish."

☀ Highlighting Development

At this stage of development, infants' memory and attention span are increasing. When they move or hit a rattle, it will make a noise. Likewise, after dropping a spoon, they notice a reaction occurs. Someone may pick it up, make a face, or even comment. As a result, infants may repeat these behaviors to get a reaction. This is how they learn about the principle of cause and effect.

VARIATION:

♡ Provide three pieces of wool yarn. Attach the fish to only one piece of yarn. Encourage the infant to find the fish.

ADDITIONAL INFORMATION:

♡ At first, infants may not look for the fish because "out of sight" means "out of mind." Encouraging them to look for the fish will assist in their developing understanding of object permanence.

🛑 At this stage of development, infants need constant supervision when involved with any toy or activity, including yarn. This is because infants have "object hunger" and typically place everything in their mouth for exploration.

What Do I Do with This?

Child's Developmental Goals

✓ To use existing cognitive schemas

✓ To develop new cognitive schemas

✓ To experience the principle of cause and effect

MATERIALS:

❏ A toy the infant has never seen before

❏ Blanket

❏ 3 or 4 pillows

PREPARATION:

♡ Select an area that you can constantly supervise. Clear this area and spread out the blanket.

♡ Place the pillows in a small semicircle on the blanket.

NURTURING STRATEGIES:

1. Sit the infant in the center of the pillows. Adjust the pillows as necessary to securely support the infant.

2. Gain the infant's attention by holding the toy in the line of vision and saying:
   "Gillian, here is a new toy. What can you do with it?"

3. Observe the infant exploring the object. Note what cognitive schemas are being used to explore the object. For example, observe to see if the object is being sucked, grasped, dropped, shaken, banged, etc.

4. To assist the infant in developing new cognitive schemas, suggest that she explore the object in a new way. For example, if the infant is sucking and grasping the object, suggest and demonstrate how it can be shaken.
   "Shake it, Gillian. Shake, shake, shake."

5. Whenever necessary, reinforce your words with actions. While gently moving the infant's arm, say:
   "Shake, shake, shake."

☀ Highlighting Development

Infants need objects and opportunities to explore the principle of cause and effect. At this stage of development they have developed a surprisingly large number of ways to explore objects using their senses: looking, tasting, touching, hearing, and smelling. Encourage them to continue adding new schemas to this existing repertoire as they explore objects.

VARIATION:

♡ Reintroduce a favorite toy. Observe the infant's exploratory behavior. How has it changed?

ADDITIONAL INFORMATION:

♡ Unless provided with new or unusual toys, the child may lose some interest; however, toys need not be expensive. Substitute boxes, wooden spoons, measuring spoons on a ring, unbreakable glasses, and cups.

♡ By manipulating objects, the infant gets to look at them from different perspectives.

 To promote safety, the objects you give to infants need to be large enough that they cannot be swallowed. They also need to be lightweight and unbreakable.

 Whenever pillows or blankets are used, constant supervision is necessary to prevent the possibility of suffocation.

4 to 6 months

Moving the Ducky

COGNITIVE

Child's Developmental Goals

✓ To use one's body for obtaining a desired effect

✓ To develop problem-solving skills

MATERIALS:

❏ Lightweight blanket

❏ Interesting infant toy such as a rubber duck

❏ Child-size table or coffee table

PREPARATION:

♡ Clear off a small table for this activity. Spread out the blanket on the table 5 to 6 inches from the edge of the place where you and the infant will be sitting.

♡ Place the toy in the middle of the blanket.

NURTURING STRATEGIES:

1. Sit down at the table and adjust your legs in a pretzel position. Next, sit the infant on your lap to provide the necessary physical support. Readjust your position as necessary, allowing the infant to sit close to the table.

2. Gain the infant's attention by pointing at the toy and describing it. Comment by saying:
   "Hector, look at the duck. You like to squeeze the duck. It makes a noise."

3. Encourage the infant to get the duck by saying:
   "Grab the blanket. Pull on the blanket. Pull. Move the duck."

4. Reinforcing your words with actions may be necessary. If so, gently place the infant's hand on the blanket while saying:
   "Touch it, Hector. Grab the blanket."
   "Now, pull it."

5. Continue providing positive reinforcement throughout the experience to maintain the infant's attention. To illustrate, say:
   "Hector, you grabbed the blanket."
   "You moved the blanket."
   "You know how to get the duck."
   "Look at you! You are squeezing the duck."

☀ Highlighting Development

Children during this stage are rapidly learning. Their development hinges on the interplay of nature and nurture. To thrive, they need stimulation, and they benefit from early interactions with parents and caregivers.

VARIATION:

♡ Repeat this activity while the infant is lying facedown on the floor. This will encourage the child to support the weight on one hand or side of his body. Moreover, in this position, the infant will be strengthening his upper body.

ADDITIONAL INFORMATION:

♡ This activity promotes high-level cognitive problem-solving skills. Infants can successfully engage in this activity with your assistance. In several months, they may be able to repeat it independently.

 Whenever pillows or blankets are used, constant supervision is necessary to prevent the possibility of suffocation.

Social

Development

FOUR to SIX MONTHS

Want to Play?

SOCIAL

4 to 6 months

Child's Developmental Goals

✓ To interact with a familiar adult

✓ To gain an adult's attention

✓ To develop a sense of trust

MATERIALS:

None

PREPARATION:

♡ Closely observe the infant for signs of interest and alertness.

NURTURING STRATEGIES:

1. The infant will signal a desire for interacting by babbling or smiling while looking for or gazing at a familiar individual.
2. When you observe these signals, position yourself so you can visually connect with the child.
3. Respond to the infant's signals by saying, for example:
   "You are telling me that you want to play."
   "You got my attention. Let's play."
   "I heard you babbling. Tell me more."
4. Continue engaging the infant by describing what is happening or by imitating the child's babble.

☀ Highlighting Development

During this stage of development, infants will usually seek out a familiar caregiver for interacting. They also enjoy social play and responding to the emotional expression of others. In fact, by five months of age, they are able to discriminate between sad and happy vocal expressions (Feldman, 1998).

VARIATION:

♡ Engage in playing by sharing a favorite toy.

ADDITIONAL INFORMATION:

♡ Infants often enjoy babbling to themselves. To gain the caregiver's attention, they may signal by smiling or squealing and using body language such as kicking their legs. This helps to further the development of their communication skills.

Making Music

Child's Developmental Goals

✓ To imitate a caregiver's behavior

✓ To continue developing a relationship with a familiar adult

MATERIALS:

❑ Blanket or mat

❑ 4 pillows or a quilt

❑ 2 wooden spoons

❑ 2 aluminum pie pans

PREPARATION:

♡ Select an area that can be constantly supervised. Clear this area and place the blanket or mat on it.

♡ If the infant can sit unassisted, the preparation is complete. If this skill has yet to be mastered, arrange the pillows in a semicircle or roll the quilt in a semicircle on the blanket or mat.

NURTURING STRATEGIES:

1. Sit the infant on the blanket or mat. Spreading the infant's legs apart into a tripod position creates a wide base of support. Adjust the pillows or quilt to ensure that the infant is securely supported in the sitting position.

2. Place the aluminum pie pan between the infant's legs while handing the child a wooden spoon.

3. Position yourself so that you can visually connect with the infant. In addition, place an aluminum pie pan in your lap.

4. Observe the infant exploring the new tools.

5. Encourage the infant to make some music with the tools you have provided. For example, say:
"Molly, bang the spoon on the plate."
"Hit them together."

6. Providing further assistance may be necessary. Reinforce your words with actions by saying:
"Molly, watch me hit them together."
"I'm banging the spoon on the plate."

7. Providing positive reinforcement usually results in a continuation of the desired behavior. For example, say enthusiastically:
"Molly, you are making music."
"You are banging the spoon on the plate."

8. Asking the infant to play will continue this interaction. Use your voice to communicate enthusiasm. For example, say:
"Let's make music together."
"Can I make music with you?"
Wait for the infant's affirmative response such as smiling or gazing at you and then join in.

☀ Highlighting Development

During this stage of development, infants will show affection for their caregivers. They will smile, laugh, babble, wiggle, and make frequent eye contact. Moreover, they will enjoy being in close proximity to you.

VARIATION:

♡ See Appendix F for a list of rhythm instruments to use with young children.

ADDITIONAL INFORMATION:

♡ Infants will be delighted in the response they receive from their actions. Therefore, this activity also fosters the development of cause and effect, which is a cognitive skill.

 Whenever pillows or blankets are used, constant supervision is necessary to prevent the possibility of suffocation.

4 to 6 months

Face to Face

SOCIAL

Child's Developmental Goals

✓ To continue developing a relationship with a familiar adult

✓ To develop a sense of trust

MATERIALS:

❑ Pillow at least 1 foot square

❑ Blanket or mat

PREPARATION:

♡ Select an area from which you can easily supervise the infant. Clear this area and lay out the blanket or mat.

♡ Place the pillow in the center of the blanket.

NURTURING STRATEGIES:

1. Lay the infant facedown on the pillow allowing his hands freedom for exploration.

2. Lie down in a prone position, placing your face 8 to 12 inches away from the infant's face.

3. Gain the infant's attention by enthusiastically saying:
   "Judd, look up. What do you see?"
   "Raise your head up."

4. When the infant looks up at you, smile to reinforce the behavior. In addition, you could say:
   "Judd, I see you looking at me."
   "You raised your head. I can see you now."

5. Continue this interaction by talking about past or future events as long as the infant communicates an interest.

Highlighting Development

The best way to help very young children grow into curious, confident, able learners is to give them warm, consistent care. Such care needs to be responsive to the infants' own needs. This will help them to form positive relationships with those who care for them (Shore, 1997).

VARIATIONS:

♡ Repeat this activity outdoors.

♡ Lie beside the infant so that you can describe and discuss items you both are looking at.

ADDITIONAL INFORMATION:

♡ Brief interactions are important since the length of an interaction should never reflect the quality. Brief, intense, one-on-one contacts can greatly assist the infant in the development of trust.

CAUTION Whenever pillows or blankets are used, constant supervision is necessary to prevent the possibility of suffocation.

SOCIAL

Floating Ball Exploration

Child's Developmental Goals

✓ To develop skills in gaining an adult's attention

✓ To develop a sense of trust

MATERIALS:

❑ Blanket or mat

❑ 4 pillows or 1 quilt

❑ 1 clear ball containing a suspended object

PREPARATION:

♡ Select and clear an area that can be constantly supervised and spread out the blanket or mat.

♡ If the infant can sit unassisted, the preparation is complete. Otherwise, arrange the pillows in a semicircle or roll the quilt and shape it in a semi-circle on the blanket or mat.

NURTURING STRATEGIES:

1. Sit the infant on the blanket or mat. Spread the infant's legs apart in a tripod position to create a wide base of support. If necessary, adjusting the pillows or quilt will ensure that the infant is securely supported in the sitting position.
2. Hand the infant the floating ball while describing it. For example, say:
   "Tisha, here is a ball. It is round."
3. Observe the infant's behaviors while exploring the ball.
4. Be alert to the infant's signals of pleasure or displeasure. Balls can easily roll out of reach and frustrate the infant. Focusing on the infant's signals will allow you to quickly respond.

5. Responding to the infant's sounds of pleasure such as babbling and laughing may reinforce these behaviors and extend the time spent exploring the floating ball. Comments include:
   "Tisha, you are watching the ball roll."
   "You are making the clown move."

☼ Highlighting Development

Balls have a lasting play value. Up to four months of age, a child will track a colorful, moving ball if it is within close proximity. From four to eight months of age, the child interacts by reaching. Moreover, the child's hands will come together in an effort to play with the ball. Through the sense of touch, the child will begin to integrate the feeling of roundness (Abrams & Kaufman, 1990).

VARIATION:

♡ Provide a favorite toy for exploring.

ADDITIONAL INFORMATION:

♡ A sense of trust is developed when caregivers are responsive to infants. Quickly responding to signals of distress and enjoyment will equally reinforce the sense of trust.

♡ If the ball rolls away, the child may become frustrated.

 Whenever pillows or blankets are used, constant supervision is necessary to prevent the possibility of suffocation.

Acting-Reacting

SOCIAL

Child's Developmental Goals

✓ To develop a self-identity
✓ To become aware of other people

MATERIALS:

❑ Large blanket or mat
❑ Activity gym

PREPARATION:

♡ Select and clear an area that can be constantly supervised. Then spread out the blanket or mat.

NURTURING STRATEGIES:

1. Lay the infant faceup under the activity gym.
2. Observe the infant exploring and interacting with the toy.
3. Describe the child's interactions. For example, say:
   "Awan, you are swatting at the bear."
   "Now you are grasping the bear."
4. Encourage the infant to explore in new ways. Suggest, for example:
   "Awan, can you move the toys like me? Watch me. I am swatting at them."
   "Now can you try swatting the toy? Good, you hit it."
5. Reinforce all attempts as well as accomplishments to foster the continuation of these behaviors.

☀ Highlighting Development

When uncomfortable or under stress, infants are quick to show signs of strain because they lack effective coping skills (Morrison, 1996). Adults must assume responsibility for exposing infants to other people and new experiences gradually. Otherwise, these new sources of stimulation may cause tension. This tension may result in the child crying. If this occurs, the child needs to be comforted.

VARIATION:

♡ Lay the infant facedown on the blanket. Then position the gym in front of the infant, allowing a new perspective. Movements required for this activity will strengthen the infant's upper arm and body muscles.

ADDITIONAL INFORMATION:

♡ The infant will probably spend more time grasping the toys hanging from the activity gym than paying attention to you. This is normal behavior for children this age. If other children or siblings are present, encourage them to interact with the child and the gym.

 Whenever pillows or blankets are used, constant supervision is necessary to prevent the possibility of suffocation.

4 to 6 months

Playing with a Friend

Child's Developmental Goals

✓ To develop a self-identity

✓ To continue developing a trusting relationship with a familiar adult

MATERIALS:

❑ Large blanket or mat

❑ 4 pillows or 1 quilt

❑ Infant toy

PREPARATION:

♡ Select an area that can be constantly supervised, clear it, and spread out the blanket or mat.

♡ If the infant can sit unassisted, the preparation is complete. Otherwise, arrange the pillows in a semicircle or roll a quilt and shape it in a semicircle on the blanket or mat.

NURTURING STRATEGIES:

1. Sit the infant on the blanket or mat. Spreading the infant's legs apart into a tripod position will create a wide base for support. Adjusting the pillows or quilt will ensure that the infant is securely supported in the sitting position. Sit next to the child in a position that will allow you to visually connect.

2. Hand the infant one of the toys while describing it. Say, for example:
   "Jing-Mei, I have an elephant for you."
   "Look at this long nose."

3. Describe what the child is doing. To illustrate, say:
   "Jing-Mei, you are holding the elephant. You are touching the trunk."

4. Continue by discussing the infant's behavior. Comments include:
   "Jing-Mei, you are playing with an elephant. You are sucking on the trunk."

5. Encourage the infant to explore the toy in new ways. Suggest, for example:
   "Jing-Mei, shake the elephant. Listen. The elephant is making a noise."

☀ Highlighting Development

When infants are born, they do not view themselves as separate from their primary caregivers. During the first year or year and a half of life, they are working on developing their self-identity. One way to foster this development is to frequently call the child by name. In addition, identifying yourself by name demonstrates that two separate and distinct people are interacting.

VARIATION:

♡ Introduce the activity in an outdoor environment, providing it is appropriate.

ADDITIONAL INFORMATION:

♡ Infants often spend more time exploring toys than gazing at you. This is normal behavior for children this age. However, if you have other children in your care, foster their involvement. This will eventually lead to development of important social skills.

 Whenever pillows or blankets are used, constant supervision is necessary to prevent the possibility of suffocation.

4 to 6 months

Riding a Blanket

SOCIAL

Child's Developmental Goals

✓ To interact with a familiar adult

✓ To develop a sense of trust

MATERIALS:

❑ Blanket

PREPARATION:

♡ Select an area that is flat and soft. Clear the area and spread out the blanket.

NURTURING STRATEGIES:

1. Lay the infant facedown on the blanket.
2. Explain to the infant what is going to happen during this activity. Say, for example:
   "Luka, let's take a ride in the blanket. You hold on. I'll pull you."
3. It may be necessary to reinforce your words with actions by helping the infant grasp the blanket.
4. Slowly begin to pull the blanket while walking backward. Respond to the infant's expressions by saying:
   "Luka, wow! You're moving!"
   "What fun! I'm pulling you on the blanket."
   "Oh, did that startle you? Should we go slower?"
5. Talk about how it feels to move in this manner. To illustrate, say:
   "Luka, what a bumpy ride."
   "It feels funny to move like this!"

☀ Highlighting Development

Exposing the child to the outdoors or a new environment is an important experience for the infant. Through outdoor activities and stroller rides, the infant is exposed to and becomes comfortable in the larger world.

VARIATIONS:

♡ Taking a stroller ride is another way to experience movement.
♡ Introduce this activity outside in a grassy area.

ADDITIONAL INFORMATION:

♡ Adjust this game to the infant's temperament. To do this, pay close attention and respond to the infant's signals. If the infant appears frightened or upset by the activity, stop immediately and soothe the child.

CAUTION Whenever pillows or blankets are used, constant supervision is necessary to prevent the possibility of suffocation.

Emotional
Development

FOUR to SIX MONTHS

Holding On

EMOTIONAL

Child's Developmental Goals

✓ To develop self-help skills
✓ To develop independence
✓ To refine a sense of self

MATERIALS:

❑ Bottle
❑ Adult-size rocking chair

PREPARATION:

♡ Heat bottle, as needed.

NURTURING STRATEGIES:

1. Sit in the rocking chair. Hold the infant in an upright position so you can visually connect.
2. Offer the infant the bottle.
3. Talk about what is happening. Comment by saying, for example:
   "Cheyenne, it's lunchtime. Time for your bottle."
   "You are hungry. You are drinking fast."
4. Encourage the infant to hold the bottle. Examples of comments to make include:
   "Cheyenne, help me. Hold your bottle."
   "Touch it with your hands."
5. It may be necessary to reinforce your words with actions. To illustrate, while moving the infant's hands to the bottle, say:
   "Cheyenne, touch the bottle. Hold it with your hands."
6. Providing positive reinforcement may encourage the infant to continue this behavior. Comments might include:
   "Cheyenne, you are doing it! You are holding your bottle."
   "What a big child!"
   "You are feeding yourself."

☼ Highlighting Development

Infants are often eager to participate in their own care. One of the first ways in which they assist is through attempting to hold the bottle during feedings. Typically, infants begin to hold the bottle independently around five to seven months of age.

VARIATION:

♡ Provide toys for the infant to grasp.

ADDITIONAL INFORMATION:

♡ By the fifth or sixth month, an infant can be provided a teething biscuit.
♡ While feeding an infant, cradle the baby in the crook of your arm so that her well-supported head is above the level of her stomach. This allows air bubbles to rise to the top of the stomach for easy burping. In addition, this may prevent earaches from milk flowing backward into the ear canal.
♡ Intimacy and trust with primary caregivers is developed during routines such as diapering and feeding.

Mirror, Mirror on the Wall

Child's Developmental Goals

✓ To express the basic emotions of interest, disgust, distress, and enjoyment

✓ To respond to the emotions of others

MATERIALS:

❑ Nonbreakable mirror

PREPARATION:

♡ Attach the mirror to the wall at a comfortable height for an adult.

NURTURING STRATEGIES:

1. Ask the infant to play by saying, for example:
   "Oded, do you want to play?"
2. If the infant indicates a desire to interact by making eye contact or smiling, pick the child up. Hold the infant so that you are facing the same way.
3. Walk over to the mirror.
4. Gain the infant's attention by gently tapping on the mirror. Say, for example:
   "I see Oded in the mirror."
   "Oded is looking at me."
5. Observe and describe the emotions being displayed by the infant. To illustrate, say:
   "You are smiling. You must be happy, Oded."
   "You are frowning. Are you sad?"

6. Display an emotional expression that the child has not shared. Verbally describe your emotional expression.

 Highlighting Development

Infants are interested in mirror images. However, they lack the cognitive structures to recognize the image as themselves (Berk, 1997). Observe. Often they will stop crying and focus on their image when held in front of the mirror.

VARIATION:

♡ While holding the child and looking in the mirror, describe each of your expressions.

ADDITIONAL INFORMATION:

♡ Infants are learning to express and regulate their emotions. They need to learn how to properly express negative emotions as well as positive emotions.

♡ The way you deal with and express your own emotions teaches the infant. Infants read and respond to your body language, tone of voice, and words. They pick up on incongruencies! Therefore, think about the emotional messages you send to infants.

4 to 6 months

I'll Help You

EMOTIONAL

Child's Developmental Goals

✓ To respond to soothing or calming behaviors of adults

✓ To learn self-soothing techniques

MATERIALS:

❑ Favorite infant toy

PREPARATION:

♡ Observe the infant for signs of distress.

NURTURING STRATEGIES:

1. When the infant displays distress, respond immediately.
2. Using your knowledge of the infant's likes and dislikes, decide on and enact behaviors that you think will be soothing or calming. For example, picking up the infant and rocking, gently bouncing, or walking may produce a calming effect.
3. Talk to the infant about feelings and emotions. To illustrate, say:
   "Frida, you are frightened. That was a loud noise."
   "You are angry."
   "You are upset."
   To accurately label the infant's emotions, you need to carefully observe the child and the environment.
4. When the infant has calmed down, provide a favorite toy. Suggest sucking, banging, or grasping the toy. All of these behaviors may have a calming effect.

5. Reinforce the infant's behavior with the toy. Say, for example:
   "Frida, you are sucking the toy. Sucking helps you calm down."

☀ Highlighting Development

The expression of happiness becomes selective around six months of age. Infants will laugh and smile more when interacting with familiar people. This is believed to be one method the infant uses for maintaining the presence of caregivers to whom they are attached.

VARIATION:

♡ Provide infants with a security item such as a blanket or pacifier to help calm them. Refer back to the Introduction (see pp. 10–11) for ways to soothe a crying child.

ADDITIONAL INFORMATION:

♡ During this time period, infants are becoming most responsive and expressive with familiar adults. Observe them and their reactions.

That's Funny!

Child's Developmental Goals

✓ To laugh aloud in response to caregiver's behavior

✓ To express the emotion of enjoyment

MATERIALS:

❑ Blanket, mat, or infant seat

PREPARATION:

♡ Select an area that can be constantly supervised. Clear this area for the blanket, mat, or infant seat.

NURTURING STRATEGIES:

1. Lay the infant faceup on the blanket or mat or securely restrain the infant in the seat using the safety strap.

2. Say the following finger play while making the motions:

Here is the beehive	(make fist)
But where are the bees?	(look in fist and shrug shoulders)
Hidden inside where nobody sees	
Here they come out of the hive	
One, two, three, four, five.	(bring out one finger at a time until reaching the number five; then tickle the infant's abdomen)

3. Smiling provides the infant with the social cue that this interaction is enjoyable. Hopefully, the infant will imitate your expression.

4. Discuss the infant's reaction to the interaction. Comments might include:
   "Mark, you are smiling. What a fun game."
   "What a laugh, Mark! You must like this game."

5. Continue this interaction as long as the infant demonstrates interest by maintaining eye contact or smiling.

☀ Highlighting Development

Infants laugh aloud or have a belly laugh around five months of age. You can respond positively to these laughs by providing lots of reinforcement such as smiling or laughing.

VARIATION:

♡ Sing a favorite song. See Appendix D for a list of additional finger plays or Appendix E for songs.

ADDITIONAL INFORMATION:

♡ Infants will imitate your expressions. Therefore, model smiling and laughing for them.

 Whenever pillows or blankets are used, constant supervision is necessary to prevent the possibility of suffocation.

That Hurts!

EMOTIONAL

Child's Developmental Goals

✓ To communicate emotions such as pain

✓ To learn techniques for controlling emotions

MATERIALS:

❑ Cold teething rings

PREPARATION:

♡ Placing sanitized teething rings in a refrigerator will keep them cool.

NURTURING STRATEGIES:

1. When an infant is crying, respond immediately. Using your knowledge of the child and the situation will help you begin to understand why the infant is crying.

2. In a calm and soothing voice, talk with the infant about her feelings. Comments include:
   "Eva, you are upset because you are wet. Let's get you changed."
   "You are in pain. You are getting a tooth."

3. If the pain is from teething, provide the infant with a cold teething ring. Discuss how this will make her mouth feel better. Say, for example:
   "Eva, chewing on this will help. It's cold."
   "New teeth hurt. Chew on this."

4. Suggest ways to deal with his emotions. Make comments such as:
   "Chewing will help the pain."
   "Crying will make you feel better, Eva."

☼ Highlighting Development

Although infants vary on the timing of tooth development, by six months of age most infants will be getting the lower front teeth. During the eruption of teeth, the child may be uncomfortable. The eruption usually causes an irritation and swelling of the gums, resulting in crankiness and fussiness. During the teething process, infants will try to bite on objects. To reduce the pain, infants may also rub at their gums. You can help them by rubbing their gums with your finger. Usually, this will help to relieve the pain.

VARIATION:

♡ Provide other sanitized infant toys for chewing.

ADDITIONAL INFORMATION:

♡ The first sound most infants make is likely to be a cry. However, infants cry for a variety of reasons. During the first six months, there typically are four types of crying. A hunger cry occurs the most frequently. Other types of cries include a cry caused by pain, a boredom cry, and an angry cry. Close observation will help you to better understand why an infant might be crying.

4 to 6 months

Helping to Undress

Child's Developmental Goals

✓ To develop self-help skills

✓ To develop independence

MATERIALS:

None

PREPARATION:

♡ Gather diapering supplies and place them on or near a changing table.

NURTURING STRATEGIES:

1. After placing the infant on the changing table, elicit the infant's assistance in undressing. For example, say:

   "Darius, I have to take off your shoes. Give me a foot."
   "I have to take off your bib overalls. Raise up."

2. You might need to reinforce your words with actions. For example, gently tap the infant's foot while saying:

   "Darius, give me your foot."

3. Praise the infant's attempts and accomplishments by commenting:

   "Darius, thank you for raising up."
   "You really helped to undress yourself."

☀ Highlighting Development

Infants find pleasure in exploring their own bodies. Watch. They may explore their ears. Over and over again, they will feel or pull on them. They also may develop an interest in exploring their nose, navel, feet, hair, and genitals.

VARIATION:

♡ Continue eliciting the infant's help when dressing and undressing before going out and after coming in from the outdoors. Emphasize different body parts such as arms, hands, legs, and feet.

ADDITIONAL INFORMATION:

♡ This activity, with repeated experience, promotes emotional as well as physical development. Infants learn body parts and can demonstrate this knowledge.

Counting

Child's Developmental Goals

✓ To laugh aloud in response to caregiver's behaviors

✓ To express the emotion of enjoyment

MATERIALS:

None

PREPARATION:

♡ Gathering diapering supplies and placing them near the changing table will free you for interacting with the child.

NURTURING STRATEGIES:

1. After diapering the child, invest quality time by interacting with the infant.
2. Ask the infant to play a counting game by saying: *"Skye, can we play a game?"*
3. If the infant indicates a desire to continue the interaction by gazing at you or smiling, begin the game. Say to the child: *"Skye, let's see how many fingers and hands you have. Let's count."*
4. Count hands first. As you count, reinforce your words with actions by touching each hand. If possible, develop a rhyme while counting.
5. Smile to convey your interest in the activity. Chances are the infant will imitate your facial expression.
6. Continue the game by counting the infant's fingers. Again, touch each finger while saying a number.

7. If this is an enjoyable activity, it may result in the infant laughing.
8. Reinforce the emotions expressed by the infant. Say, for example: *"Skye, you like this game." "What a laugh. You are having fun!"*

☀ Highlighting Development

Infants typically begin laughing between two and four months of age. Laughter at first is elicited only in response to stimulation such as loud sounds or tickling. Social and visual stimuli based on cognitive interpretation beginning at six months of age will foster laughter in the infants. Action book games and toys such as a jack-in-the-box will also promote laughter (Snow, 1998).

VARIATION:

♡ Reinforce the names of body parts by counting the infant's feet, toes, ears, and nose.

ADDITIONAL INFORMATION:

♡ Share your enthusiasm. The success of this activity greatly depends on your facial expressions. Infants will look to you for cues for reacting.

♡ In this situation, counting promotes the development of rhythm rather than the development of numerical skills.

References

Abrams, B. W., & Kaufman, N. A. (1990). *Toys for early childhood development.* West Nyack, NY: The Center for Applied Research in Education.

Baillargeon, R. (1994). How do infants learn about the physical world? *Current Directions in Psychological Science,* 133–140.

Baron, N. S. (1992). *Growing up with language: How children learn to talk.* Reading, MA: Addison-Wesley.

Bentzen, W. R. (2001). *Seeing young children: A guide to observing and recording behavior* (4th ed.). Clifton Park, NY: Delmar Learning.

Berk, L. E. (1997). *Child development* (4th ed.). Boston: Allyn & Bacon.

Feldman, R. S. (1998). *Child Development.* Upper Saddle River, NJ: Prentice Hall.

Fogel, A. (2001). *Infancy* (2nd ed.). Belmont, CA: Wadsworth.

Gandini, L., & Goldhaber, J. (2001). Two reflections about documentation. In L. Gandini and C. Pope Edwards (Eds.), *Bambini: The Italian approach to infant/toddler care* (pp. 124–145). New York: Teachers College Press.

Helm, J. H., Beneke, S., & Steinheimer, K. (1998). *Windows on learning: Documenting young children's work.* New York: Teachers College Press.

Izard, C. E. (1991). *The psychology of emotions.* New York: Plenum.

Junn, E., & Boyatzis, C. J. (1998). *Child growth and development.* Guilford, CT: Dushken/McGraw Hill.

Kail, R. U. (1998). *Children and their development.* Upper Saddle River, NJ: Prentice Hall.

Kostelnik, M., Stein, L., Whiren, A. P., Soderman, A. K., & Gregory, K. (2002). *Guiding children's social development.* Clifton Park, NY: Delmar Learning.

Kratcoski, A. M., & Katz, K. B. (1998). Conversing with young language learners in the classroom. *Young Children, 53*(3), 30–33.

Leach, P. (1992). *Your baby and child: From birth to age five.* New York: Alfred A. Knopf.

Morrison, G. S. (1996). *Early childhood education today.* Upper Saddle River, NJ: Merrill.

Shore, R. (1997). *Rethinking the brain: New insights into early development.* New York: Families and Work Institute.

Snow, C. W. (1998). *Infant development* (2nd ed.). Upper Saddle River, NJ: Prentice Hall.

Zigler, E., & Stevenson, M. F. (1993). *Children in a changing world: Development and social issues* (2nd ed.). Pacific Grove, CA: Brooks/Cole.

Appendix A
Books for Infants

Young children need to be immersed in a literacy-rich environment. A foundation for reading success begins as early as the first few months of life. Exposure to books and caring adults nourishes literacy development. Books and oral language are tools to help infants become familiar with language. Young children enjoy handling books and listening to stories. Infants enjoy the visual and auditory stimulation of having books read to them over and over again.

Books help very young children by:

♡ Developing visual discrimination skills

♡ Developing visual memory skills

♡ Developing listening skills

♡ Developing auditory memory skills

♡ Presenting new and interesting information

♡ Introducing new vocabulary

♡ Stimulating new thoughts and ideas

♡ Helping children learn book-handling skills such as turning pages and reading text versus pictures

Books that are developmentally appropriate for infants are abundant. Some of the best examples feature various physical formats combined with clearly developed concepts or a simple story and distinctive art or photographic work.

Features of books for babies and infants include a scaled-down size appropriate for manipulation with small hands and for lap reading. Pages are either soft for safety or thick for sturdiness and ease of turning. Many books have a wipe-clean finish and rounded corners for safety. Formats include cloth, vinyl, and floatable bathtub books in chunky sizes. The content is concept-oriented with clear pictures or photographs, usually including babies or objects relating to a baby's life.

SELECTING BOOKS

Careful consideration should be given to selecting age-appropriate books for young children. When choosing books, begin by looking for award winners. You can ask the librarian at your local library to give you a list of award-winning picture books; likewise, do not hesitate to ask the salesperson at a local bookstore to provide this information. Chances are they will have a list of these award-winning books or can complete a computer search to obtain this information for you. On-line merchants should also be able to provide you this information.

You should also review the illustrations for size and quality before selecting a picture book. Study them carefully. You will notice a wide variety of illustration types in books for infants. There are photographs, watercolors, line drawings, and collages. As you review books, remember that infants need to have large, realistic illustrations. Realistic illustrations serve two purposes: They help the young children maintain their interest in the book and they help develop concept formation.

Other questions beside award-winning status and quality of illustrations to ask yourself while evaluating books for infants include:

♡ Is the book developmentally appropriate for the child or group of children?

♡ Does the book have visual appeal?

♡ Are the pages thick, durable, and easy to clean?

♡ Are the illustrations large and brightly colored?

♡ Do the illustrations contain pictures of familiar objects, routines, or people?

♡ Does the story reflect the children's own experiences?

♡ Is the vocabulary appropriate?

SUGGESTIONS FOR READING TO INFANTS

There are seven steps to making reading an enjoyable and educational experience for infants.

♡ Get comfortable! Sit on a couch, in a rocking chair, or on the floor with your back against a wall. Hold the child in your lap or snuggle close to a small group of children.

♡ Read slowly, allowing plenty of time for children to look at the illustrations. This increases the pleasure and enjoyment derived from books for *everyone* involved.

♡ Ask questions to engage children in conversation. The experience should be as much about speaking skills as listening skills for young children.

♡ Pause to encourage children to read along with you. You will find that infants will coo or babble. These experiences also serve to reinforce the development of turn-taking skills.

♡ Read for as long as children enjoy it. Forcing young children to remain in a situation when they are finished only serves to diminish their "love of books."

♡ Share your enthusiasm for the book through your voice and facial expressions. Children learn to love books when an adult shares their own enjoyment.

CLOTH BOOKS

Animal Play. Dorling Kindersley, 1996.
Briggs, Raymond. *The Snowman.* Random House, 1993.
Cousins, Lucy. My First Cloth Book series. Candlewick Press.
    Flower in the Garden. 1992.
    Hen on the Farm. 1992.
    Kite in the Park. 1992.
    Teddy in the House. 1992.
Harte, Cheryl. *Bunny Rattle.* Random House, 1989. (Has a rattle in it)
    Ducky Squeak. Random House, 1989. (Has a squeaker in it)
Hill, Eric. *Clothes-Spot Cloth Book.* Putnam, 1993.
    Play-Spot Cloth Book. Putnam, 1993.
My First Notebook. Eden International Ltd. (Has a rattle inside and plastic spiral rings.)
Pienkowski, Jan. Jan Pienkowski's First Cloth Book series. Little Simon.
    Animals. 1995.
    Friends. 1995.
    Fun. 1996.
    Play. 1995.
Pienkowski, Jan. *Bronto's Brunch.* Dutton Books, 1995. (Has detachable pieces. Ages 3+)
    Good Night, Moo. Dutton Books, 1995. (Has detachable pieces. Ages 3+)
Potter, Beatrix. Beatrix Potter Cloth Books. Frederick Warne & Co.
    My Peter Rabbit Cloth Book. 1994.
    My Tom Kitten Cloth Book. 1994.
Pudgy Pillow Books. Grosset & Dunlap.
    Baby's Animal Sounds. 1989.
    Baby's Little Engine That Could. 1989.
    Barbaresi, Nina. *Baby's Mother Goose.* 1989.
    Ulrich, George. *Baby's Peek A Boo.* 1989.
Tong, Willabel L. Cuddly Cloth Books. Andrews & McMeel.
    Farm Faces. 1996.
    My Pets. 1997.
    My Toys. 1997.
    Zoo Faces. 1997.
Tucker, Sian. My First Cloth Book series. Simon & Schuster.
    Quack, Quack. 1994.
    Rat-A-Tat-Tat. 1994.
    Toot Toot. 1994.
    Yum Yum. 1994.

VINYL COVER AND BATH BOOKS

Bracken, Carolyn. *Baby's First Rattle: A Busy Bubble Book.* Simon & Schuster, 1984.

De Brunhoff, Laurent. *Babar's Bath Book.* Random House, 1992.
Hill, Eric. *Spot's Friends.* Putnam, 1984.
    Spot's Toys. Putnam, 1984.
    Sweet Dreams, Spot. Putnam, 1984.
Hoban, Tana. *Tana Hoban's Red, Blue, Yellow Shoe.* Greenwillow Books, 1994.
    Tana Hoban's What Is It? Greenwillow Books, 1994.
I. M. Tubby. *I'm a Little Airplane.* Simon & Schuster, 1982. (Shape book)
    I'm a Little Choo Choo. Simon & Schuster, 1982. (Shape book)
    I'm a Little Fish. Simon & Schuster, 1981. (Shape book)
My First Duck. Dutton, 1996. (Playskool shape book)
Nicklaus, Carol. *Grover's Tubby.* Random House/Children's Television Workshop, 1992.
Potter, Beatrix. Beatrix Potter Bath Books series. Frederick Warne & Co.
    Benjamin Bunny. 1994.
    Jemima Puddle-Duck. 1988.
    Mr. Jeremy Fisher. 1989.
    Peter Rabbit. 1989.
    Tom Kitten, Mittens, and Moppet. 1989.
Reichmeier, Betty. *Potty Time.* Random House, 1988.
Smollin, Michael J. *Ernie's Bath Book.* Random House/Children's Television Workshop, 1982.
Tucker, Sian. Sian Tucker Bath Books series. Simon & Schuster.
    Animal Splash. 1995.
    Splish Splash. 1995.

TOUCH AND FEEL BOOKS

Carter, David A. *Feely Bugs.* Little Simon, 1995.
Chang, Cindy. *Good Morning Puppy.* Price Stern Sloan, 1994.
    Good Night Kitty! Price Stern Sloan, 1994.
Demi, Hitz. *Downy Duckling.* Grosset & Dunlap, 1988.
    Fluffy Bunny. Grosset & Dunlap, 1987.
Hanna, Jack. *Let's Go to the Petting Zoo with Jungle Jack.* Doubleday, 1992.
Hill, Eric. *Spot's Touch and Feel Day.* Putnam, 1997.
Kunhardt, Dorothy. *Pat the Bunny.* Western Publishing, 1968.
Kunhardt, Dorothy & Edith. *Pat the Cat.* Western Publishing, 1984.
    Pat the Puppy. Western Publishing, 1993.
Lodge, J. *Patch and His Favorite Things.* Harcourt Brace, 1996.
    Patch in the Garden. Harcourt Brace, 1996.
Offerman, Lynn. *Puppy Dog's Special Friends.* Joshua Morris Publishing, 1998.
Scarry, Richard. *Richard Scarry's Egg in the Hole Book.* Golden Books, 1997.
Witte, Pat & Eve. *The Touch Me Book.* Golden Books, 1946.

CHUNKY AND CHUBBY BOOKS

Barton, Byron. Chunky Board Book series. HarperCollins.
  Boats. 1994.
  Planes. 1994.
  Trains. 1994.
Bond, Michael. *Paddington at the Seashore.* HarperCollins, 1992.
Brown, Marc. Chunky Flap Book series. Random House.
  Arthur Counts. 1998.
  Arthur's Farm Tales. 1998.
  D.W.'s Color Book. 1997.
  Where Is My Frog? 1991.
  Where's Arthur's Gerbil? 1997.
  Where's My Sneaker? 1991.
Cowley, Rich. *Snap! Snap! Buzz Buzz.* Firefly Books, 1996.
Dunn, Phoebe. *Baby's Animal Friends.* Random House, 1988.
  Farm Animals. Random House, 1984.
Freeman, Don. *Corduroy's Toys.* Viking, 1985.
Fujikawa, Gyo. *Good Night, Sleep Tight! Shhh . . .* Random House, 1990. (Chunky shape)
Hill, Eric. Spot Block Book series. Putnam.
  Spot's Favorite Baby Animals. 1997.
  Spot's Favorite Numbers. 1997.
  Spot's Favorite Words. 1997.
Hirashima, Jean. *ABC.* Random House, 1994. (Chunky shape)
Ingle, Annie. *Zoo Animals.* Random House, 1992.
Loehr, Mallory. *Trucks.* Random House, 1992. (Chunky shape)
Marzollo, Jean. *Do You Know New?* HarperCollins, 1997.
McCue, Lisa. *Little Fuzzytail.* Random House, 1995. (Chunky Peek a Board Book)
Miller, Margaret. Super Chubby Book series. Simon & Schuster.
  At the Shore. 1996.
  Family Time. 1996.
  Happy Days. 1996.
  Let's Play. 1997.
  My Best Friends. 1996.
  Water Play. 1996.
  Wheels Go Round. 1997.
Oxenbury, Helen. *Helen Oxenbury's Little Baby Books.* Candlewick Press, 1996.
  Boxed set includes: *I Can; I Hear; I See; I Touch.*
  Pienkowski, Jan. Nursery Board Book series. Simon & Schuster.

Colors. 1987.	*Sizes.* 1991.
Faces. 1991.	*Stop Go.* 1992.
Food. 1991.	*Time.* 1991.
Homes. 1990.	*Yes No.* 1992.

Ricklen, Neil. Super Chubby Book series. Simon & Schuster.

Baby Outside. 1996.	*Baby's Good Night.* 1992.
Baby's 123. 1990.	*Baby's Neighborhood.* 1994.
Baby's ABC. 1997.	*Baby's Playtime.* 1994.
Baby's Big & Little. 1996.	*Baby's Toys.* 1997.
Baby's Clothes. 1997.	*Baby's Zoo.* 1992.
Baby's Friends. 1997.	*Daddy and Me.* 1997.
Baby's Home. 1997.	*Mommy and Me.* 1997.
Baby's Good Morning. 1992.	

Ross, Anna. *Knock Knock, Who's There?* Random House/Children's Television Workshop, 1994. (Chunky flap)
Ross, Katharine. *The Little Quiet Book.* Random House, 1989.
Santoro, Christopher. *Open the Barn Door.* Random House, 1993. (Chunky flap)
Scarry, Richard. *Richard Scarry's Lowly Worm Word Book.* Random House, 1981.
  Richard Scarry's Cars and Trucks from A–Z. Random House, 1990. (Chunky shape)
Shappie, Trisha Lee. *Where Is Your Nose?* Scholastic, 1997.
Smollin, Michael. *In & Out, Up & Down.* Random House, Children's Television Network, 1982.
  Ernie & Bert Can . . . Can You? Random House, Children's Television Network, 1982.
Snapshot Chubby Book series. Dorling Kindersley.
  ABC. 1994.
  Colors. 1994.
  My Home. 1995.
  My Toys. 1995.
  Shapes. 1994.
Van Fleet, Matthew. *Fuzzy Yellow Ducklings.* Dial Books, 1995.
Wik, Lars. *Baby's First Words.* Random House, 1985.

BOARD BOOKS

Alborough, Jez. *Ice Cream Bear.* Candlewick Press, 1997.
  It's the Bear. 1994.
  My Friend Bear. 1998.
  Bare Bear. Random House, 1984.
  Running Bear. 1985.
Bang, Molly. *Ten, Nine, Eight.* First Tupelo Board Book edition. Tupelo Books, 1998.
Boynton, Sandra. Boynton Board Book series. Simon & Schuster.
  But Not the Hippopotamus. 1995.
  Blue Hat, Green Hat. 1995.
  Doggies, A Counting and Barking Book. 1995.
  Going to Bed Book. 1995.
  Moo, Baa, La La La. 1995.
  Opposites. 1995.
  Hey! Wake Up! Workman Publishing, 2000.
Brett, Jan. *The Mitten: A Ukrainian Folktale.* Putnam, 1996. (Board book)
Brown, Margaret Wise. First Board Book editions. HarperCollins.

Child's Good Night Book. Pictures by Jean Charlot. 1996.

Goodnight Moon. Pictures by Clement Hurd. 1991.

Runaway Bunny. Pictures by Clement Hurd, 1991.

Carle, Eric. First Board Book editions. HarperCollins.

Do You Want to Be My Friend? 1995.

The Mixed-Up Chameleon. 1998.

The Secret Birthday Message. 1998.

The Very Quiet Cricket. Putnam, 1997.

Have You Seen My Cat? First Little Simon Board Book edition. Simon & Schuster, 1996.

The Very Hungry Caterpillar. First Board Book edition. Philomel Books, 1994.

Carle, Eric. Play-and-Read Books. Cartwheel Books.

Catch the Ball. 1998.

Let's Paint a Rainbow. 1998.

What's for Lunch? 1998.

Carlstrom, Nancy White. Illus. by Bruce Degen. Simon & Schuster. (Board book)

Bizz Buzz Chug-A-Chug: Jesse Bear's Sounds. 1997.

Hooray for Blue: Jesse Bear's Colors. 1997.

I Love You, Mama, Any Time of Year. Jesse Bear Board Book. 1997.

I Love You, Papa, In All Kinds of Weather. Jesse Bear Board Book. 1997.

Jesse Bear, What Will You Wear? 1996.

Choosing Colors. Photos by Sandra Lousada. Dutton Children's Books/Playskool, 1995. (Board book)

Cohen, Miriam. *Backpack Baby.* Star Bright Books, 1999.

Say Hi, Backpack Baby: A Backpack Baby Story. 2000.

Cousins, Lucy. Dutton Children's Books. (Board book)

Humpty Dumpty and Other Nursery Rhymes. 1996.

Jack & Jill and Other Nursery Rhymes. 1996.

Little Miss Muffet and Other Nursery Rhymes. 1997.

Wee Willie Winkie and Other Nursery Rhymes. 1997.

Day, Alexandra. *Good Dog, Carl.* First Little Simon Board Book edition. Simon & Schuster, 1996.

Degen, Bruce. *Jamberry.* First Board Book edition. HarperCollins, 1995.

dePaola, Tomie. *Strega Nona.* First Little Simon Board Book edition. Simon & Schuster, 1997.

Ehlert, Lois. *Color Farm.* First Board Book edition. HarperCollins, 1997.

Color Zoo. First Board Book edition. HarperCollins, 1997.

Eating the Alphabet. First Red Wagon Books. Harcourt Brace, 1996.

Fleming, Denise. *Count!* First Board Book edition. Henry Holt, 1997.

Mama Cat Has Three Kittens. 1998.

The Everything Book. 2000.

Hoban, Tana. *Black on White.* Greenwillow Books, 1993.

Red, Blue, Yellow Shoe. 1986.

What Is It? 1985.

White on Black. 1993.

Hooker, Yvonne. Illus. by Carlo A. Michelini. Poke and Look books. Grosset & Dunlap.

One Green Frog. 1989.

Wheels Go Round. 1989.

Hopp, Lisa. *Circus of Colors.* Illus. by Chiara Bordoni. Poke and Look book. Grosset & Dunlap, 1997.

Isadora, Rachel. *I Touch.* Greenwillow Books, 1991. (Board book)

Keats, Ezra Jack. *The Snowy Day.* Viking, 1996. (Board book)

Kirk, David. *Miss Spider's Tea Party: The Counting Book.* First Board Book edition. Callaway & Kirk/Scholastic Press, 1997.

Lewison, Wendy. *Nighty Night.* Illus. by Giulia Orecchia. Poke and Look book. Grosset & Dunlap, 1992.

Lundell, Margaretta. *Land of Colors.* Illus. by Nadia Pazzaglia. Poke and Look book. Grosset & Dunlap, 1989.

Lundell, Margo. *What Does Baby See?* Illus. by Roberta Pagnoni. Poke and Look book. Putnam & Grosset, 1990.

Martin, Bill. Illus. by Eric Carle. First Board Book editions. Henry Holt.

Brown Bear, Brown Bear, What Do You See? 1996.

Polar Bear, Polar Bear, What Do You Hear? 1997.

Martin, Bill, & Archambault, John. *Chicka Chicka ABC.* Illus. by Lois Ehlert. First Little Simon Board Book edition. Simon & Schuster, 1993.

Marzollo, Jean. *I Spy Little Book.* Illus. by Walter Wick. Scholastic, 1997. (Board book)

I Spy Little Animals. Photos by Walter Wick. 1998. (Board book)

Do You Know New? HarperCollins, 1997.

Mama, Mama. HarperFestival, 1999.

Papa, Papa. 2000.

Pretend You're a Cat. Dial Books, 1990.

McBratncy, Sam. *Guess How Much I Love You.* First Board Book edition. Candlewick Press, 1996.

McMullan, Kate. *If You Were My Bunny.* Illus. by David McPhail. First Board Book edition. Cartwheel Books, 1998.

Miller, Margaret. *Baby Faces.* Little Simon, 1998.

What's On My Head? 1998.

Miller, Virginia. *Be Gentle!* Candlewick Press, 1997.

Eat Your Dinner! 1992.

Go to Bed! 1993.

In a Minute! 2000.

On Your Potty! 1998.

Ogden, Betina, illus. *Busy Farmyard.* So Tall board book. Grosset & Dunlap, 1995.

Omerod, Jan. *101 Things to Do With a Baby.* Mulberry Books, 1993.

Opie, Iona Archibald. Illus. by Rosemary Wells. Mother Goose Board Book series. Candlewick Press.

Pussycat, Pussycat and Other Rhymes. 1997.

Humpty Dumpty and Other Rhymes. 1997.

Little Boy Blue and Other Rhymes. 1997.

Wee Willie Winkie and Other Rhymes. 1997.

Oxenbury, Helen. Baby Board Books. Wanderer Books.

Dressing. 1981.
Family. 1981.
Friends. 1981.
Playing. 1981.
Working. 1981.
Pfister, Marcus. Board book. North–South Books.
    Hopper. 1998.
    Hopper Hunts for Spring. 1998.
    The Rainbow Fish. 1996.
    Rainbow Fish to the Rescue. 1998.
Pinkney, Andrea & Brian. *Pretty Brown Face.* Harcourt Brace, 1997.
Piper, Watty. *The Little Engine That Could.* Illus. by Christina Ong. Platt & Munk, 1991.
Potter, Beatrix. *The Tale of Peter Rabbit.* Illus. by Florence Graham. Pudgy Pal Board Book. Grosset & Dunlap, 1996.
Pragoff, Fiona. Fiona Pragoff Board Books. Simon & Schuster.
    Baby Days. 1995.
    Baby Plays. 1995.
    Baby Ways. 1994.
    It's Fun to Be One. 1994.
    It's Fun to Be Two. 1994.
Raffi. First Board Book editions. Crown Publishers.
    Baby Beluga. Illus. by Ashley Wolff. 1997.
    Wheels on the Bus. Illus. by Sylvie Kantorovitz Wickstrom. 1998.
Rathmann, Peggy. *Good Night, Gorilla.* Board book. Putnam, 1996.
Reasoner, Charles, & Hardt, Vicky. *Alphabite! A Funny Feast from A to Z.* Board book. Price Stern Sloan, 1989.
Rey, H. A. & Margret. Board books. Houghton Mifflin, 1998.
    Curious George and the Bunny. 1998.
    Curious George's ABC's. 1998.
    Curious George's Are You Curious? 1998.
    Curious George's Opposites. 1998.

Rosen, Michael. *We're Going on a Bear Hunt.* Illus. by Helen Oxenbury. First Little Simon Board Book edition. Simon & Schuster, 1997.
Seuss, Dr. Bright and Early Board Book series. Random House.
    Dr. Seuss's ABC. 1996.
    The Foot Book. 1997.
    Mr. Brown Can Moo, Can You? 1996.
    The Shape of Me and Other Stuff. 1997.
    There's a Wocket in My Pocket. 1996.
Snapshot Board Book series. Dorling Kindersley.
    All about Baby by Stephen Shott. 1994.
    Baby and Friends by Paul Bricknell. 1994.
    Good Morning, Baby by Jo Foord, et al. 1994.
    Good Night, Baby by Mike Good & Stephen Shott. 1994.
Waddell, Martin. *Owl Babies.* Illus. by Patrick Benson. First Board Book edition. Candlewick Press, 1992.
Wells, Rosemary. *Max's Birthday.* Max Board Book. Dial Books for Young Readers, 1998.
    Old MacDonald. Bunny Reads Back Board Book. Scholastic, 1998.
Wilkes, Angela. *My First Word Board Book.* Dorling Kindersley, 1997.
Williams, Sue. *I Went Walking.* Illus. by Julie Vivas. First Red Wagon Books edition. Harcourt Brace, 1996.
Williams, Vera B. *More, More, More Said the Baby.* First Tupelo Board Book edition. William Morrow, 1997.
Wood, Jakki. *Moo Moo, Brown Cow.* Illus. by Rog Bonner. First Red Wagon Board book. Harcourt Brace, 1996.
Ziefert, Harriet. Board Book. Dorling Kindersley.
    Food! 1996.
    Let's Get Dressed. Illus. by Susan Baum. 1997.
    My Clothes. 1996.

Appendix B

Criteria for Selecting Materials and Equipment for Children

Even though most materials and equipment appear safe, you will find that infants have an uncanny ability to find and remove parts. This may pose a threat. Therefore, to reduce safety hazards, you must constantly check and observe. When purchasing or choosing materials and equipment to use with infants, carefully determine if the items promote safety and development by using the following checklist.

SAFETY	Yes	No
A. Is it unbreakable?		
B. Is it durable?		
C. Is it washable?		
D. Is it too large to be swallowed?		
E. Is it free of removable parts?		
F. Is it free of sharp edges?		
G. Is it constructed from nontoxic materials?		
H. Is it free of pinching cracks?		
I. Is it suitable for the available space?		
PROMOTES DEVELOPMENT		
A. Is it developmentally appropriate?		
B. Does it challenge the child's development?		
C. Does it complement existing materials or equipment?		
D. Does it teach multiple skills?		
E. Does it involve the child?		
F. Is it nongender biased?		
G. Does it promote a multicultural perspective?		
H. Does it promote nonviolent play?		

Appendix C

Materials and Equipment for Promoting Optimal Development

Materials and equipment play a major role in promoting an infant's development, as well as provide enjoyment.

Materials and Equipment to Promote Development for Infants

animal, toy
baby lotion
balls
bells
blanket or mat
blocks for building, lightweight
books (black & white and picture books—cardboard, cloth, and/or vinyl)
carpet pieces
cars, large toy
cassettes or compact discs, a variety of music: jazz, lullabies, classical, etc.
couch or sturdy furniture
crayons, large
diaper-changing table
dishes, nonbreakable (e.g., cups, spoons, plates)
doll accessories: blanket, bed, clothes

dolls, multiethnic
doughs and clays
elastic bands
fill and dump toys
glider
high chair
household items (e.g., pots, pans, wooden spoons, metal or plastic bowls, laundry baskets)
infant seat
infant stroller
large beads to string
mirrors (unbreakable)
mobile
musical instruments, child-size
nesting cups
pacifier
pails and shovels
paintbrushes
pictures of infants
pillows

pop-up toys
props to accompany finger plays
puppets
puzzles with large pieces
push and pull toys
rattles, different sizes, shapes, weights, and textures
riding toys
rocking chair
rubber toys
squeeze toys
stacking rings
stroller
stuffed animals
sun catchers
tape or compact disc recorder
teething rings
towels
toy telephones
wheeled toys
wind chimes

Appendix D
Favorite Finger Plays, Nursery Rhymes, and Chants

Finger plays, nursery rhymes, and chants help infants to develop social interaction skills, listening and auditory memory skills, expressive language skills, and concept formation. They also help infants become aware of their body parts and see themselves as persons who can do things.

Finger plays use a variety of actions and words together; some involve whole body actions. An example is the finger play "This Little Piggy," which is a favorite for infants. The younger the child, the shorter and simpler the rhyme and the body action need to be. For these children, larger body parts are more suitable. The young child will join you visually and participate in the actions before learning the words. Typically, after repeated exposure, the toddlers will gradually learn some of the words while others may learn the entire finger play. This appendix contains examples of finger plays, nursery rhymes, and chants that children may enjoy. Note that finger plays can be an important technique for teaching "Who am I?"; young children particularly enjoy these activities when their names are included.

ANIMALS

Can you hop like a rabbit?
   (*suit actions to words*)
Can you jump like a frog?
Can you walk like a duck?
Can you run like a dog?
Can you fly like a bird?
Can you swim like a fish?
And be still like a good child?
As still as this?

BODY TALK

When I smile, I tell you that I'm happy.
   (*point to the mouth*)
When I frown I tell you that I am sad.
   (*pull down corners of the mouth*)
When I raise my shoulders and tilt my head I tell you,
   "I don't know."
   (*raise shoulders, tilt head, raise hands, and shake head*)

BRUSHING TEETH

I move the toothbrush back and forth.
   (*pretend to brush teeth*)
I brush all of my teeth.
I swish the water to rinse them and then
   (*puff out cheeks to swish*)
I look at myself and smile.
   (*smile at one another*)

THE CHIMNEY

Here is the chimney,
   (*make hand into a fist with thumb inside*)
Here is the top.
   (*place other hand on top of fist*)

Open the lid.
   (*remove top hand*)
Out Santa will pop.
   (*pop up thumb*)

A CIRCLE

Around in a circle we will go.
Little tiny baby steps make us go very slow.
And then we'll take some great giant steps,
As big as they can be.
Then in a circle we'll stand quietly.

CIRCUS CLOWN

I'd like to be a circus clown
And make a funny face,
   (*make a funny face*)
And have all the people laugh at me
As I jump around the place.
   (*act silly and jump around*)

CLAP YOUR HANDS 1

Clap your hands 1, 2, 3.
   (*suit actions to words*)
Clap your hands just like me.
Roll your hands 1, 2, 3.
Roll your hands just like me.

CLAP YOUR HANDS 2

Clap, clap, clap your hands,
As slowly as you can.
Clap, clap, clap your hands,
As fast as you can.

CLOCKS

*(rest elbows on hips; extend forearms and index fingers up
    and move arms sideways slowly and rhythmically)*
Big clocks make a sound like
Tick, Tock, Tick, Tock.
    (speak slowly)
Small clocks make a sound like
    (move arms faster)
Tick, tock, tick, tock.
And the very tiny clocks make a sound
    (move still faster)
Like tick, tick, tock, tock.
Tick, tock, tick, tock, tick, tock.

FIVE LITTLE PUMPKINS

*(hold up five fingers and bend them down one
    at a time as verse progresses)*
Five little pumpkins sitting on a gate;
The first one said, "My it's getting late."
The second one said, "There are witches in the air."
The third one said, "But we don't care."
The fourth one said, "Let's run, let's run."
The fifth one said, "It's Halloween fun."
"Wooooooo" went the wind,
    (sway hand through the air)
And out went the lights.
    (loud clap)
These five little pumpkins ran fast out of sight.
    (place hands behind back)

FRIENDS

I like my friends,
So when we are at play,
I try to be very kind
And nice in every way.

GOBBLE, GOBBLE

A turkey is a funny bird,
His head goes wobble, wobble.
    (place hands together and move back and forth)
And he knows just one word,
Gobble, gobble, gobble.

GRANDMA'S SPECTACLES

*(bring index finger and thumb together and place against face
    as if wearing glasses)*
These are Grandma's spectacles.
This is Grandma's hat.
    (bring fingertips together in a peak over head)
This is the way she folds her hands,
    (clasp hands together)
And lays them in her lap.
    (lay hands in lap)

HERE IS A BALL

Here is a ball,
    (touch fingers of both hands to form a ball)
Here is a bigger ball,
    (bow the arms with fingers touching to form a second ball)
And here is the biggest ball of all.
    (extend arms and do not touch fingers)
Now let us count the balls we made:
    One,
    Two,
    Three
    *(repeat making the balls to reinforce the concepts by
    showing the increasing size)*

HICKORY, DICKORY, DOCK

Hickory, dickory, dock.
The mouse ran up the clock.
The clock struck one, the mouse ran down,
Hickory, dickory, dock.

I LOOKED INSIDE MY MIRROR

I looked inside my mirror
To see what I could see.
It looks like I am happy today,
Because that smiling face is me.

I LOVE MY FAMILY

Some families are large.
    (spread arms out wide)
Some families are small.
    (bring arms close together)
But I love my family
    (cross arms over chest)
Best of all!

JACK AND JILL

Jack and Jill went up a hill
To fetch a pail of water.
Jack fell down and broke his crown
And Jill fell tumbling after.

JACK-IN-THE-BOX

Jack-in-the-box
Sit so still
    (squat or stoop down, placing hands over head as a cover)
Won't you come out?
Yes, I will!
    (open hands and jump up)

LITTLE JACK HORNER

Little Jack Horner
Sat in a corner
Eating a Christmas pie.
  (*pretend you're eating*)
He put in his thumb,
  (*point thumb down*)
And pulled out a plum
  (*point thumb up*)
And said, "What a good boy am I!"
  (*say out loud*)

LITTLE MISS MUFFET

Little Miss Muffet
Sat on a tuffet
Eating her curds and whey.
Along came a spider
And sat down beside her
And frightened Miss Muffet away!

RING AROUND THE ROSIE

(*teacher and children hold hands and walk around
  in a circle*)
Ring around the rosie,
A pocket full of posies,
Ashes, ashes,
We all fall down.
  (*everyone falls to the ground*)

THE MONKEY

The monkey claps, claps, claps his hands.
  (*clap hands*)
The monkey claps, claps his hands.
  (*clap hands*)
Monkey see, monkey do,
The monkey does the same as you.
  (*use pointer finger*)

The monkey pats his arm, pats his arm.
  (*pat arm*)
The monkey pats his arm, pats his arm.
  (*pat arm*)
Monkey see, monkey do,
The monkey does the same as you.
  (*use pointer finger*)

The monkey touches his head, touches his head.
  (*touch head*)
The monkey touches his head, touches his head.
  (*touch head*)
Monkey see, monkey do,
The monkey does the same as you.
  (*use pointer finger*)

The monkey gives a big smile, gives a big smile.
  (*smile big*)
The monkey gives a big smile, gives a big smile.
  (*smile big*)

Monkey see, monkey do,
The monkey does the same as you.
  (*use pointer finger*)

The monkey crawls all around, crawls all around.
  (*get down on hands and knees and crawl*)
The monkey crawls all around, crawls all around.
  (*get down on hands and knees and crawl*)
Monkey see, monkey do,
The monkey does the same as you.
  (*use pointer finger*)

THE MUFFIN MAN

Oh, do you know the muffin man,
The muffin man, the muffin man?
Oh, do you know the muffin man
Who lives on Drury Lane?
Yes, I know the muffin man,
The muffin man, the muffin man.
Oh, yes, I know the muffin man
Who lives on Drury Lane.

THE MULBERRY BUSH

(*Since this is a lengthy finger play, begin with just a verse or
two and then gradually individually add the remaining verses
as the toddlers gain proficiency.*)

Here we go 'round the mulberry bush,
The mulberry bush, the mulberry bush.
Here we go 'round the mulberry bush,
So early in the morning.

This is the way we wash our clothes,
Wash our clothes, wash our clothes.
This is the way we wash our clothes,
So early Monday morning.

This is the way we iron our clothes,
Iron our clothes, iron our clothes.
This is the way we iron our clothes,
So early Tuesday morning.

This is the way we scrub our clothes,
Scrub our clothes, scrub our clothes.
This is the way we scrub our clothes,
So early Wednesday morning.

This is the way we mend our clothes,
Mend our clothes, mend our clothes.
This is the way we mend our clothes,
So early Thursday morning.

This is the way we sweep the house,
Sweep the house, sweep the house.
This is the way we sweep the house,
So early Friday morning.

This is the way we bake our bread,
Bake our bread, bake our bread.
This is the way we bake our bread,
So early Saturday morning.

This is the way we go to church,
Go to church, go to church.
This is the way we go to church,
So early Sunday morning.

(The children can join hands with you and skip around in a circle. They can act out the words of the song beginning with the second verse. If church is inappropriate for Sunday, another activity can be substituted such as barbeque, play ball, mow the lawn, etc.)

MY PUPPY

I like to pet my puppy.
  (pet puppy)
He has such nice soft fur.
  (pet puppy)
And if I don't pull his tail
  (pull tail)
He won't say, "Grr!"
  (make face)

MY RABBIT

My rabbit has two big ears
  (hold up index and middle fingers for ears)
And a funny little nose.
  (join the other fingers for a nose)
He likes to nibble carrots
  (separate thumb from other two fingers)
And he hops wherever he goes.
  (move whole hand jerkily)

MY TOOTHBRUSH

I have a little toothbrush.
  (use pointer finger)
I hold it very tight.
  (make hand into fist.)
I brush my teeth each morning,
And then again at night.
  (use pointer finger and pretend to brush)

MY TURTLE

This is my turtle.
  (make fist; extend thumb)
He lives in a shell.
  (hide thumb in fist)
He likes his home very well.
He pokes his head out when he wants to eat.
  (extend thumb)
And pulls it back when he wants to sleep.
  (hide thumb in fist)

OLD KING COLE

Old King Cole was a merry old soul
  (lift elbows up and down)
And a merry old soul was he.
  (nod head)

He called for his pipe.
  (clap two times)
He called for his bowl.
  (clap two times)
And he called for his fiddlers three.
  (clap two times then pretend to play violin)

ONE, TWO, BUCKLE MY SHOE

One, two, buckle my shoe.
  (count on fingers as verse progresses)
Three, four, shut the door.
  (suit actions to words)
Five, six, pick up sticks.
Seven, eight, lay them straight.
Nine, ten, a big tall hen.

OPEN, SHUT THEM

Open, shut them.
  (suit actions to words)
Open, shut them.
Open, shut them.
Give a little clap.
Open, shut them.
Open, shut them.
Open, shut them.
Put them in your lap.
Creep them, creep them
Right up to your chin.
Open up your little mouth,
But do not put them in.
Open, shut them.
Open, shut them.
Open, shut them.
To your shoulders fly,
Then like little birdies
Let them flutter to the sky.
Falling, falling almost to the ground,
Quickly pick them up again and turn
Them round and round.
Faster, faster, faster.
Slower, slower, slower.
  (repeat first verse)

PAT-A-CAKE

Pat-a-cake, pat-a-cake, baker's man.
Bake me a cake as fast as you can!
  (clap hands together lightly)
Roll it
  (roll hands)
And pat it
  (touch hands together lightly)
And mark it with a *B*
  (write B in the air)
And put it in the oven for baby and me.
  (point to baby and yourself)

POPCORN CHANT I

Popcorn, popcorn
Hot, hot, hot
Popcorn, popcorn
Pop, pop, pop.

POPCORN CHANT 2

Popcorn, popcorn
In a pot
What'll happen when you get hot?
Boom! Pop. Boom! Pop. Pop.
That's what happens when you get hot!

POPCORN CHANT 3

Popcorn, popcorn
In a dish
How many pieces do you wish?
1, 2, 3, 4
Eat those up and have some more!

RAINDROPS

Rain is falling down.
Rain is falling down.
    (*raise arm, flutter fingers to the ground, tapping the floor*)
Pitter-patter
Pitter-patter
Rain is falling down.

READY NOW, LET'S GO

I am a little kitty,
I have to tippy toe.
Come and do it with me.
Ready now, let's go.
    (*take tiny steps*)

I am a little rabbit.
I love to hop, hop, hop.
Come and do it with me.
It's fun we will never stop.
    (*hop around*)

I am a big bird.
I love to fly around using my wings.
Come and do it with me.
Ready now? Let's go.
    (*use arms as wings to fly*)

I am a great big elephant.
I take big steps so slow.
I'd love to have you join me.
Ready now? Let's go
    (*take slow, big steps*)

I am a little puppy.
I love to run and run.
Come and do it with me.
We will have such fun.
    (*run like a puppy*)

RIGHT HAND, LEFT HAND

This is my right hand,
I'll raise it up high.
    (*raise the right hand up high*)
This is my left hand.
I'll touch the sky.
    (*raise the left hand up high*)
Right hand,
    (*show right palm*)
Left hand,
    (*show left palm*)
Roll them around
    (*roll hands over and over*)
Left hand,
    (*show palm*)
Right hand,
    (*show palm*)
Pound, pound, pound.
    (*hit fists together*)

SEE, SEE, SEE

See, see, see
    (*shade eyes with hands*)
Three birds are in a tree.
    (*hold up three fingers*)
One can chirp
    (*point to thumb*)
And one can sing
    (*point to index finger*)
One is just a tiny thing.
    (*point to middle finger, then rock baby bird in arms*)
See, see, see
Three birds are in a tree.
    (*hold up three fingers*)

STAND UP TALL

Stand up tall
Hands in the air.
Now sit down
In your chair.
Clap your hands
And make a frown.
Smile and smile.
Hop like a clown.

TEAPOT

I'm a little teapot,
  (*place right hand on hip, extend left, palm out*)
Short and stout.
Here's my handle.
And here's my spout.
When I get all steamed up, I just shout:
"Tip me over, and pour me out."
  (*bend to left*)
I can change my handle
  (*place left hand on hip and extend right hand out*)
And my spout.
"Tip me over, and pour me out."
  (*bend to the right*)

TEDDY BEAR

Teddy bear, teddy bear, turn around.
Teddy bear, teddy bear, touch the ground.
Teddy bear, teddy bear, climb the stairs.
Teddy bear, teddy bear, jump into bed.
Teddy bear, teddy bear, turn out the lights.
Teddy bear, teddy bear, blow a kiss.
Teddy bear, teddy bear, say goodnight.
Goodnight.

TEN LITTLE DUCKS

Ten little ducks swimming in the lake.
  (*move ten fingers as if swimming*)
Quack! Quack!
  (*snap fingers twice*)
They give their heads a shake.
  (*shake fingers*)
Glunk! Glunk! Go go little frogs.
  (*two claps of hands*)
And away to their mothers,
The ten ducks run.
  (*move hands in running motion from front to back*)

TEN LITTLE FINGERS

I have ten little fingers and ten little toes.
  (*children point to portions of body as they repeat words*)
Two little arms and one little nose.
One little mouth and two little ears.
Two little eyes for smiles and tears.
One little head and two little feet.
One little chin, that makes _____ complete.

THIS LITTLE PIGGY

This little piggy went to market.
  (*point to one finger at a time*)
This little piggy stayed home.
This little piggy had roast beef.
This little piggy had none.
This little piggy cried, "Wee, wee, wee."
And ran all the way home.

THREE FROGS

Three little frogs
  (*hold up three fingers of left hand*)
Asleep in the sun.
  (*fold them over*)
We'll creep up and wake them.
  (*make creeping motion with fingers of right hand*)
Then we will run.
  (*hold up three fingers while right hand runs away*)

THREE LITTLE DUCKIES

Three little duckies
  (*hold up three fingers*)
Swimming in the lake.
  (*make swimming motions*)
The first ducky said,
  (*hold up one finger*)
"Watch the waves I make."
  (*make wave motions*)
The second ducky said,
  (*hold up two fingers*)
"Swimming is such fun."
  (*smile*)
The third ducky said,
  (*hold up three fingers*)
"I'd rather sit in the sun."
  (*turn face to sun*)
Then along came a motorboat.
With a Pop! Pop! Pop!
  (*clap three times*)
And three little duckies
Swam away from the spot.
  (*put three fingers behind back*)

THREE LITTLE MONKEYS

Three little monkeys jumping on the bed.
  (*hold up three fingers*)
One fell off and bumped his head.
Mama called the doctor and the doctor said,
No more monkeys jumping on the bed.
  (*shake pointer finger as if scolding*)

Two little monkeys jumping on the bed,
  (*hold up two fingers*)
One fell off and bumped his head.
Mama called the doctor and the doctor said,
No more monkeys jumping on the bed.
  (*shake pointer finger as if scolding*)

One little monkey jumping on the bed.
  (*hold up one finger*)
He fell off and bumped his head.
Mama called the doctor and the doctor said,
No more jumping on the bed.
  (*shake pointer finger as if scolding*)

TWO LITTLE APPLES

(*hold hands above head, form circles with thumb
   and forefinger of each hand*)
Away up high in the apple tree,
Two red apples smiled at me.
   (*smile*)
I shook that tree as hard as I could.
   (*put hands out as if on tree—shake*)
And down they came.
   (*hands above head and lower to ground*)
And ummmmm were they good!
   (*rub tummy*)

TWO LITTLE BLACKBIRDS

Two little blackbirds sitting on a hill.
   (*show two fingers*)
One named Jack.
   (*hold up one finger on right hand*)
One named Jill.
   (*hold up one finger on the left hand*)
Fly away Jack.
   (*move right hand behind back*)
Fly away Jill.
   (*move the left hand behind back*)
Come back Jack.
   (*return right hand*)
Come back Jill.
   (*return left hand*)
(Children's names can be substituted for Jack and Jill in
   this finger play.)

TWO LITTLE KITTENS

(*hold up two fingers, cup hands together to form a ball*)
Two little kittens found a ball of yarn
As they were playing near a barn.
   (*bring hands together pointed upward for barn*)
One little kitten jumped in the hay,
   (*hold up one finger, make jumping then wiggling motion*)
The other little kitten ran away.
   (*make running motion with other hand*)

ZOO ANIMALS

This is the way the elephant goes.
   (*clasp hands together, extend arms, move back and forth*)
With a curly trunk instead of a nose.
The buffalo, all shaggy and fat.
Has two sharp horns in place of a hat.
   (*point to forehead*)
The hippo with his mouth so wide
Let's see what's inside.
   (*hands together and open wide and close them*)
The wiggly snake upon the ground
Crawls along without a sound.
   (*weave hands back and forth*)
But monkey see and monkey do is the
funniest animal in the zoo.
   (*place thumbs in ears and wiggle fingers*)

Appendix E

Songs

Music is a universal language and a natural form of expression for children of all ages. Infants need to have a wide variety of music experiences that are casual and spontaneous. They enjoy lullabies that are slow, soft, and soothing. In addition to lullabies, classical, folk and music from different ethnic and cultural groups should all be included. Children like songs about animals and familiar objects, which tell a story and contain frequent repetition. Choose simple songs with a strong melody that represent their age, abilities, and interests. Chances are children will more easily remember these songs. While singing, remember to convey enthusiasm.

Music is a valuable experience for young children. They enjoy listening to music while engaged in activities and napping. Music promotes the development of listening skills and builds vocabulary. It is a tool that provides an opportunity for learning new concepts such as up/down, fast/slow, heavy/light, and loud/soft. Music releases tension, stimulates the imagination, and promotes the development of auditory memory skills.

ALL ABOUT ME

Brushing Teeth
(Tune: "Mulberry Bush")
This is the way we brush our teeth,
Brush our teeth, brush our teeth.
This is the way we brush our teeth,
So early in the morning.

Good Morning
Good morning to you.
Good morning to you.
We're all in our places,
With bright shining faces,
Good morning to you.

ANIMALS

The Animals on the Farm
(Tune: "The Wheels on the Bus")
The cows on the farm go moo, moo, moo,
Moo, moo, moo, moo, moo, moo.
The cows on the farm go moo, moo, moo,
All day long.

The horses on the farm go nay, nay, nay,
Nay, nay, nay, nay, nay, nay.
The horses on the farm go nay, nay, nay,
All day long.

OTHER VERSES:
Pigs—oink
Sheep—baa
Chicken—cluck
Turkeys—gobble

The Ants Go Marching One by One
The ants go marching one by one.
Hurrah! Hurrah!
The ants go marching one by one.
Hurrah! Hurrah!
The ants go marching one by one.

The little one stops to suck her thumb
And they all go marching,
Down in the ground
To get out of the rain.
Boom Boom Boom

OTHER VERSES:
Two by two
The little one stops to tie his shoe
Three by three
The little one stops to scratch her knee
Four by four
The little one stops to shut the door
Five by five
The little one stops to wave goodbye.

Circus
(Tune: "Did You Ever See a Lassie")
Let's pretend that we are clowns, are clowns, are clowns.
Let's pretend that we are clowns.
We'll have so much fun.
We'll put on our makeup and make people laugh hard.
Let's pretend that we are clowns.
We'll have so much fun.

Let's pretend that we are elephants, are elephants, are elephants.
Let's pretend that we are elephants.
We'll have so much fun.
We'll sway back and forth and stand on just two legs.
Let's pretend that we are elephants.
We'll have so much fun.

Let's pretend that we are on a trapeze, a trapeze, a trapeze.
Let's pretend that we are on a trapeze.
We'll have so much fun.
We'll swing high and swoop low and make people shout "oh"!
Let's pretend that we are on a trapeze.
We'll have so much fun!

Easter Bunny
(Tune: "Ten Little Indians")
Where, oh, where is the Easter Bunny,
Where, oh, where is the Easter Bunny,
Where, oh, where is the Easter Bunny,
Early Easter morning?

Find all the eggs and put them in a basket,
Find all the eggs and put them in a basket,
Find all the eggs and put them in a basket,
Early Easter morning.

Itsy Bitsy Spider
The itsy bitsy spider went up the water spout
Down came the rain and washed the spider out
Out came the sun and dried up all the rain
And the itsy bitsy spider went up the spout again.
(This is also a popular finger play.)

Kitty
(Tune: "Bingo")
I have a cat. She's very shy.
But she comes when I call Kitty
K-I-T-T-Y
K-I-T-T-Y
K-I-T-T-Y
and Kitty is her name-o.

(Variation: Let children think of other names.)

Old MacDonald Had a Farm
Old MacDonald had a farm,
E-I-E-I-O.
And on his farm he had some cows,
E-I-E-I-O.
With a moo, moo here and a moo, moo there,
Here a moo, there a moo, everywhere a moo, moo.
Old MacDonald had a farm,
E-I-E-I-O.

OTHER VERSES:
Sheep—baa, baa
Pigs—oink, oink
Ducks—quack, quack
Chickens—chick, chick

Two Little Black Bears
(Tune: "Two Little Blackbirds")
Two little black bears sitting on a hill
One named Jack, one named Jill.
Run away Jack
Run away Jill.
Come back Jack
Come back Jill.
Two little black bears sitting on a hill
One named Jack, one named Jill.

CLEANUP SONGS

Cleanup Time 1
(Tune: "London Bridge")
Cleanup time is already here,
Already here, already here.
Cleanup time is already here,
Already here.

Cleanup Time 2
(Tune: "Hot Cross Buns")
Cleanup time.
Cleanup time.
Put all of the toys away.
It's cleanup time.

Do You Know What Time It Is?
(Tune: "The Muffin Man")
Oh, do you know what time it is,
What time it is, what time it is?
Oh, do you know what time it is?
It's almost cleanup time.
   (Or, it's time to clean up.)

A Helper I Will Be
(Tune: "The Farmer in the Dell")
A helper I will be.
A helper I will be.
I'll pick up the toys and put them away.
A helper I will be.

It's Cleanup Time
(Tune: "Looby Loo")
It's cleanup time at the preschool.
It's time for boys and girls
To stop what they are doing.
And put away their toys.

Oh, It's Cleanup Time
(Tune: "Oh, My Darling Clementine")
Oh, it's cleanup time,
Oh, it's cleanup time,
Oh, it's cleanup time right now.
It's time to put the toys away,
It is cleanup time right now.

Passing Around
(Tune: "Skip to My Loo")
Brad, take a napkin and pass them to Sara.
Sara, take a napkin and pass them to Tina.
Tina, take a napkin and pass them to Eric.
Passing around the napkins.

(Fill in the appropriate child's name and substitute for "napkin" any object that needs to be passed at mealtime.)

Put Your Coat On
(Tune: "Oh, My Darling Clementine")
Put your coat on.
Put your coat on.
Put your winter coat on now.
We are going to play outside.
Put your coat on right now.
(*Change "coat" to any article of clothing.*)

This Is the Way
(Tune: "Mulberry Bush")
This is the way we pick up our toys,
Pick up our toys, pick up our toys.
This is the way we pick up our toys,
At cleanup time each day.
(*Substituting "before bedtime" opposed to "cleanup time" could modify this song.*)

Time to Clean up
(Tune: "Are You Sleeping?")
Time to clean up.
Time to clean up.
Everybody help.
Everybody help.
Put the toys away, put the toys away.
Then sit down. (*Or, then come here.*)
(*Specific toys can be mentioned in place of "toys."*)

We're Cleaning Up Our Room
(Tune: "The Farmer in the Dell")
We're cleaning up our room.
We're cleaning up our room.
We're putting all the toys away.
We're cleaning up our room.

FAVORITES

London Bridge
London Bridge is falling down,
Falling down, falling down.
London Bridge is falling down.
My fair lady.

Twinkle, Twinkle, Little Star
Twinkle, twinkle, little star,
How I wonder what you are!
Up above the world so high,
Like a diamond in the sky.
Twinkle, twinkle, little star,
How I wonder what you are!

Where Is Thumbkin?
Where is thumbkin?
Where is thumbkin?
Here I am,
Here I am.
How are you today, sir?
Very well, I thank you.
Fly away, fly away.

OTHER VERSES:
Pointer
Tall man
Ring man
Pinky

FEELINGS

Feelings
(Tune: "Twinkle, Twinkle, Little Star")
I have feelings.
You do, too.
Let's all sing about a few.
I am happy. (*smile*)
I am sad. (*frown*)
I get scared. (*wrap arms around self*)
I get mad. (*sneer and wrinkle nose*)
I am proud of being me. (*hands on hips*)
That's a feeling, too, you see.
I have feelings. (*point to self*)
You do, too. (*point to someone else*)
We just sang about a few.

If You're Happy and You Know It
If you're happy and you know it
Clap your hands.
  (*clap twice*)
If you're happy and you know it
Clap your hands.
  (*clap twice*)
If you're happy and you know it
Then your face will surely show it.
If you're happy and you know it
Clap your hands.
  (*clap twice*)

If you're sad and you know it
Say boo-hoo.
  (*rub your eyes*)
If you're sad and you know it
Say boo-hoo.
  (*rub your eyes*)
If you're sad and you know it
Then your face will surely show it.
If you're sad and you know it
Say boo-hoo.
  (*rub your eyes*)

If you're mad and you know it
Wrinkle your nose.
  (*wrinkle nose*)
If you're mad and you know it
Wrinkle your nose.
  (*wrinkle nose*)
If you're mad and you know it
Then your face will surely show it.
If you're mad and you know it
Wrinkle your nose.
  (*wrinkle nose*)

PEOPLE

Are You Sleeping?
Are you sleeping?
Are you sleeping?
Brother John, brother John,
Morning bells are ringing,
Morning bells are ringing.
Ding, ding, dong!
Ding, ding, dong!

Do You Know This Friend of Mine?
(Tune: "The Muffin Man")
Do you know this friend of mine,
This friend of mine,
This friend of mine?
Do you know this friend of mine?
Her name is _____.
Yes, we know this friend of yours,
This friend of yours,
This friend of yours.
Yes, we know this friend of yours.
Her name is _____.

The Muffin Man
Oh, do you know the muffin man,
The muffin man, the muffin man?
Oh, do you know the muffin man,
Who lives on Drury Lane?

Oh, yes we know the muffin man,
The muffin man, the muffin man.
Oh, yes we know the muffin man,
Who lives on Drury Lane.

Oh, how do you know the muffin man,
The muffin man, the muffin man?
Oh, how do you know the muffin man,
Who lives on Drury Lane.

Cause [Papaw] is the muffin man,
The muffin man, the muffin man.
[Pawpaw] is the muffin man,
Who lives on Drury Lane.

(Substitute names of other males who are important in the child's life, such as Daddy or Uncle Todd.)

This Old Man
This old man
He played one
He played knick knack on a drum
With a knick knack, paddy whack
Give the dog a bone
This old man came rolling home.

OTHER VERSES:
He played two
He played knick knack on my shoe.
He played three
He played knick knack on a tree
He played four
He played knick knack at my door
He played five
He played knick knack on a hive.

TRANSPORTATION

Row, Row, Row, Your Boat
Row, row, row your boat.
Gently down the stream.
Merrily, merrily, merrily, merrily,
Life is but a dream.

The Wheels on the Bus
The wheels on the bus go round and round.
Round and round, round and round.
The wheels on the bus go round and round.
All around the town.

OTHER VERSES:
The wipers on the bus go swish, swish, swish.
The doors on the bus go open and shut.
The horn on the bus goes beep, beep, beep.
The driver on the bus says, "Move on back."
The people on the bus go up and down.

Appendix F
Rhythm Instruments

Using rhythm instruments is a method of teaching young children to express themselves. Rhythm instruments can be common household objects or purchased through school supply stores or catalogs. Examples include:

Commercially Purchased	Household Items
Drums	Pots
Jingle sticks	Pans
Cymbals	Lids
Rattles	Wooden spoons
Wrist bells	Aluminum pie pans
Shakers	Metal whisks
Maracas	Plastic bowls
Sandpaper blocks	

You can also improvise and construct these instruments—save cans, cardboard tubes that have plastic lids from nuts, chips, and coffee. These items can be used as drums. If you place noise-making objects inside the cans or tubes, they can be used as shakers. However, make sure that you secure the lid using a high-quality adhesive tape that children cannot remove.

Appendix G
Resources Related to Infants

The authors and Delmar make every effort to ensure that all Internet resources are accurate at the time of printing. However, due to the fluid, time-sensitive nature of the Internet, we cannot guarantee that all URLs and Web site addresses will remain current for the duration of this edition.

The American Montessori Society Bulletin
American Montessori Society (AMS)
281 Park Avenue South, 6th Floor
New York, NY 10010-6102
(212) 358-1250; (212) 358-1256 FAX
www.amshq.org

Babybug
Cricket Magazine Group
PO Box 7437
Red Oak, IA 51591-2437
(800) 827-0227
www.babybugmag.com

The Black Child Advocate
National Black Child Development Institute
(NBCDI)
1101 15th Street NW, Suite 900
Washington, DC 20005
(202) 833-2220; (202) 833-8222 FAX
www.nbcdi.org

Child and Youth Quarterly
Human Sciences Press
233 Spring Street, Floor 5
New York, NY 10013-1522
(212) 620-8000

Child Development and Child Development Abstracts and Bibliography
Society for Research in Child Development
University of Michigan
505 East Huron, Suite 301
Ann Arbor, MI 48104-1567
(734) 998-6578; (734) 998-6569 FAX
www.srcd.org

Child Health Alert
PO Box 610228
Newton Highlands, MA 02161
(781) 239-1762
ericps.ed.uiuc.edu/npin/nls/chalert.html

Childhood Education; Journal of Research in Early Childhood Education
Association for Childhood Education
International (ACEI)
17904 Georgia Avenue; Suite 215
Olney, MD 20832
(301) 570-2111; (301) 570-2212 FAX
www.udel.edu/bateman/acei

Child Welfare
Child Welfare League of America (CWLA)
440 First Street NW, 3rd Floor
Washington, DC 20001-2085
(202) 638-2952; (202) 638-4004 FAX
www.cwla.org

Children Today
Superintendent of Documents
U.S. Government Printing Office
Washington, DC 20402
www.access.gpo.gov

Early Childhood Education Journal
Human Sciences Press
233 Spring Street, Floor 5
New York, NY 10013-1522
(212) 620-8000
www.wkap.nl/journalhome.htm/1082-3301

Developmental Psychology
American Psychological Association
750 First Street NE
Washington, DC 20002-4242
(202) 336-5500
www.apa.org

Dimensions of Early Childhood
Southern Association for Children Under Six
Box 56130 Brady Station
Little Rock, AR 72215
(800) 305-7322; (501) 227-5297 FAX

Early Child Development and Care
Gordon and Breach Publishing
Box 32160
Newark, NJ 07102
(800) 545-8398
www.gbhap.com

Earlychildhood NEWS
Earlychildhood.com
2 Lower Ragsdale, Suite 125
Monterey, CA 93940
(831) 333-5501; (800) 627-2829;
(831) 333-5510 FAX
www.earlychildhood.com

Early Childhood Research Quarterly
National Association for the Education of Young
Children (NAEYC)
1509 16th Street NW
Washington, DC 20036-1426
(202) 232-8777; (202) 328-1846 FAX
www.naeyc.org

Educational Leadership
Association for Supervision and Curriculum
Development (ASCD)
1703 North Beauregard Street
Alexandria, VA 22311-1714
(703) 578-9600; (800) 933-ASCD;
(703) 575-5400 FAX
www.ascd.org

Educational Researcher
American Educational Research Association
(AERA)
1230 17th Street NW
Washington, DC 20036
(202) 223-9485; (202) 775-1824 FAX
www.aera.net

ERIC/EECE
University of Illinois
Children's Research Center
51 Gerty Drive
Champaign, IL 61820-7469
http://ericps.ed.uiuc.edu/eece

Exceptional Children
Council for Exceptional Children
1110 North Glebe Road, Suite 300
Arlington, VA 22201-5704
(703) 620-3660; (888) CEC-SPED;
(703) 264-9494 FAX
www.cec.sped.org

Gifted Child Quarterly
National Association for Gifted Children
1707 L Street NW, Suite 550
Washington, DC 20036
(202) 785-4268
www.nagc.org

Instructor
Scholastic, Inc.
555 Broadway
New York, NY 10012
www.scholastic.com/instructor

Journal of Family and Consumer Sciences
American Association of Family and Consumer
Services (AAFCS)
1555 King Street
Alexandria, VA 22314
(703) 706-4600; (703) 706-4663 FAX
www.aafcs.org

Young Children
National Association for the Education of Young
Children (NAEYC)
1509 16th Street NW
Washington, DC 20036-1426
(202) 232-8777; (202) 328-1846 FAX
www.naeyc.org

Other information may be obtained through various
professional organizations.

The following groups may be able to provide you with
other resources:

American Association for Gifted Children
Box 90270
Durham, NC 27708-0270
www.aagc.org

*American Association of Family and Consumer Services
(AAFCS)*
1555 King Street
Alexandria, VA 22314
(703) 706-4600; (703) 706-4663 FAX
www.aafcs.org

American Montessori Association (AMS)
281 Park Avenue South, 6th Floor
New York, NY 10010
(212) 358-1250; (212) 358-1256 FAX
www.amshq.org

*Association for Childhood Education International
(ACEI)*
17904 Georgia Avenue, Suite 215
Olney, MD 20832
(301) 570-2111; (800) 423-3563;
(301) 570-2212 FAX
www.udel.edu/bateman/acei

*Association for Supervision and Curriculum
Development (ASCD)*
    1703 North Beauregard Street
    Alexandria, VA 22311-1714
    (703) 578-9600; (800) 933-ASCD;
    (703) 575-5400 FAX
    www.ascd.org

*Canadian Association for the Education of Young
Children (CAYC)*
    612 West 23rd Street
    Vancouver, BC V7M 2C3
    www.cayc.ca

Children's Defense Fund
    25 E Street NW
    Washington, DC 20001
    (202) 628-8787
    www.childrensdefense.org

Child Welfare League of America
    440 First Street NW, 3rd Floor
    Washington, DC 20001-2085
    (202) 638-2952; (202) 638-4004 FAX
    www.cwla.org

Council for Exceptional Children
    1110 North Glebe Road, Suite 300
    Arlington, VA 22201-5704
    (703) 620-3660; (888) CEC-SPED;
    (703) 264-9494 FAX
    www.cec.sped.org

International Reading Association
    800 Barksdale Road
    PO Box 8139
    Newark, DE 19714-8139
    (302) 731-1600; (302) 731-1057 FAX
    www.reading.org

*National Association for the Education of Young
Children (NAEYC)*
    1509 16th Street NW
    Washington, DC 20036-1426
    (202) 232-8777; (202) 328-1846 FAX
    www.naeyc.org

National Association for Gifted Children
    1707 L Street NW, Suite 550
    Washington, DC 20036
    (202) 785-4268
    www.nagc.org

National Black Child Development Institute (NBCDI)
    1101 15th Street NW, Suite 900
    Washington, DC 20005
    (202) 833-2220; (202) 833-8222 FAX
    www.nbcdi.org

National Committee to Prevent Child Abuse
    2950 Tennyson Street
    Denver, CO 80212
    (303) 433-2451; (303) 433-9701 FAX
    www.childabuse.org

National Education Association (NEA)
    1201 16th Street NW
    Washington, DC 20036
    (202) 833-4000
    www.nea.org

Society for Research in Child Development
    University of Michigan
    505 East Huron, Suite 301
    Ann Arbor, MI 48104-1567
    (734) 998-6578; (734) 998-6569 FAX
    www.srcd.org

Appendix H
Developmental Checklist

Child's Name: _____

Observer's Name: _____

Observation Date: _____

PHYSICAL DEVELOPMENT	OBSERVED	
Birth to Three Months	**Date**	**Comments**
Acts reflexively—sucking, stepping, rooting		
Swipes at objects in front of body, uncoordinated		
Holds head erect and steady when lying on stomach		
Lifts head and shoulders		
Rolls from side to back		
Follows moving objects with eyes		
Four to Six Months		
Holds cube in hand		
Reaches for objects with one hand		
Rolls from back to side		
Reaches for objects in front of body, coordinated		
Sits with support		
Transfers objects from hand to hand		
Grabs objects with either hand		
Sits in tripod position using arms for support		
Seven to Nine Months		
Sits independently		
Stepping reflex returns, so that child bounces when held on a surface in a standing position		
Leans over and reaches when in a sitting position		
Gets on hands and knees but may fall forward		
Crawls		
Pulls to standing position		
Claps hands together		
Stands with adult's assistance		
Learns pincer grasp, using thumb with forefinger to pick up objects		
Uses finger and thumb to pick up objects		
Brings objects together with banging noises		

The developmental milestones listed are based on universal patterns of when various traits emerge. Because each child is unique certain traits may develop at an earlier or later age.

PHYSICAL DEVELOPMENT	OBSERVED	
Ten to Twelve Months	Date	Comments
Supports entire body weight on legs		
Walks when hands are held		
Cruises along furniture or steady objects		
Stands independently		
Walks independently		
Crawls up stairs or steps		
Voluntarily releases objects held in hands		
Has good balance when sitting; can shift positions without falling		
Takes off shoes and socks		
Thirteen to Eighteen Months		
Builds tower of two cubes		
Turns the pages of a cardboard book two or three at a time		
Scribbles vigorously		
Walks proficiently		
Walks while carrying or pulling a toy		
Walks up stairs with assistance		
Nineteen to Twenty-Four Months		
Walks up stairs independently, one step at a time		
Jumps in place		
Kicks a ball		
Runs in a modified fashion		
Shows a decided preference for one hand		
Completes a three-piece puzzle with knobs		
Builds a tower of six cubes		
Twenty-Five to Thirty-Six Months		
Maneuvers around obstacles in a pathway		
Runs in a more adult-like fashion; knees are slightly bent, arms move in the opposite direction		
Walks down stairs independently		
Marches to music		
Uses feet to propel wheeled riding toys		
Rides a tricycle		
Usually uses whole arm movements to paint or color		
Throws a ball forward, where intended		
Builds tower using eight or more blocks		
Imitates drawing circles and vertical and horizontal lines		
Turns pages in book one by one		
Fingers work together to scoop up small objects		
Strings large beads on a shoelace		

Additional Observations for Physical Development

The developmental milestones listed are based on universal patterns of when various traits emerge. Because each child is unique certain traits may develop at an earlier or later age.

LANGUAGE AND COMMUNICATION DEVELOPMENT (continued)	OBSERVED	
Birth to Three Months	Date	Comments
Communicates with cries, grunts, and facial expressions		
Prefers human voices		
Coos		
Laughs		
Smiles and coos to initiate and sustain interactions with caregiver		
Four to Six Months		
Babbles spontaneously		
Acquires sounds of native language in babble		
Canonical, systematic consonant-vowel pairings; babbling occurs		
Participates in interactive games initiated by adults		
Takes turns while interacting		
Seven to Nine Months		
Varies babble in loudness, pitch, and rhythm		
Adds *d, t, n,* and *w* to repertoire of babbling sounds		
Produces gestures to communicate often by pointing		
May say *mama* or *dada* but does not connect words with parents		
Ten to Twelve Months		
Uses preverbal gestures to influence the behavior of others		
Demonstrates word comprehension skills		
Waves good-bye		
Speaks recognizable first word		
Initiates familiar games with adults		
Thirteen to Eighteen Months		
Has expressive vocabulary of 10 to 20 words		
Engages in "jargon talk"		
Engages in telegraphic speech by combining two words together		
Experiences a burst of language development		
Comprehends approximately 50 words		
Nineteen to Twenty-Four Months		
Continues using telegraphic speech		
Able to combine three words		
Talks, 25 percent of words being understandable		
Refers to self by name		

The developmental milestones listed are based on universal patterns of when various traits emerge. Because each child is unique certain traits may develop at an earlier or later age.

LANGUAGE AND COMMUNICATION DEVELOPMENT	OBSERVED	
Nineteen to Twenty-Four Months (continued)	Date	Comments
Joins three or four words into a sentence		
Comprehends approximately 300 words		
Expressive language includes a vocabulary of approximately 250 words		
Twenty-Five to Thirty-Six Months		
Continues using telegraphic speech combining three or four words		
Speaks in complete sentences following word order of native language		
Displays effective conversational skills		
Refers to self as *me* or *I* rather than by name		
Talks about objects and events not immediately present		
Uses grammatical markers and some plurals		
Vocabulary increases rapidly, up to 300 words		
Enjoys being read to if allowed to participate by pointing, talking, and turning pages		

Additional Observations for Language and Communication Development

COGNITIVE DEVELOPMENT	OBSERVED	
Birth to Three Months	Date	Comments
Cries for assistance		
Acts reflexively		
Prefers to look at patterned objects, bull's-eye, horizontal stripes, and the human face		
Imitates adults' facial expressions		
Searches with eyes for sources of sounds		
Begins to recognize familiar people at a distance		
Discovers and repeats bodily actions such as sucking, swiping, and grasping		
Discovers hands and feet as extension of self		

The developmental milestones listed are based on universal patterns of when various traits emerge. Because each child is unique certain traits may develop at an earlier or later age.

COGNITIVE DEVELOPMENT (continued)		OBSERVED	
Four to Six Months	Date		Comments
Recognizes people by their voice			
Enjoys repeating acts, such as shaking a rattle, that produce results in the external world			
Searches with eyes for source of sounds			
Enjoys watching hands and feet			
Searches for a partially hidden object			
Uses toys in a purposeful manner			
Imitates simple actions			
Explores toys using existing schemas such as sucking, banging, grasping, shaking, etc.			
Seven to Nine Months			
Enjoys looking at books with familiar objects			
Distinguishes familiar from unfamiliar faces			
Engages in goal-directed behavior			
Anticipates events			
Finds objects that are totally hidden			
Imitates behaviors that are slightly different than those usually performed			
Begins to show interest in filling and dumping containers			
Ten to Twelve Months			
Solves sensorimotor problems by deliberately using schemas, such as shaking a container to empty its contents			
Points to body parts upon request			
Drops toys intentionally and repeatedly looks in the direction of the fallen object			
Waves good-bye			
Shows evidence of stronger memory capabilities			
Follows simple, one-step directions			
Categorizes objects by appearance			
Looks for objects hidden in a second location			
Thirteen to Eighteen Months			
Explores properties of objects by acting on them in novel ways			
Solves problems through trial and error			
Experiments with cause-and-effect relationships such as turning on televisions, banging on drums, etc.			
Plays body identification games			
Imitates novel behaviors of others			
Identifies family members in photographs			

The developmental milestones listed are based on universal patterns of when various traits emerge. Because each child is unique certain traits may develop at an earlier or later age.

Nineteen to Twenty-Four Months	Date	Comments
Points to and identifies objects on request, such as when reading a book, touring, etc.		
Sorts by shapes and colors		
Recognizes self in photographs and mirror		
Demonstrates deferred imitation		
Engages in functional play		
Finds objects that have been moved while out of sight		
Solves problems with internal representation		
Categorizes self and others by gender, race, hair color, etc.		
Twenty-Five to Thirty-Six Months		
Uses objects for purposes other than intended		
Uses private speech while working		
Classifies objects based on one dimension, such as toy cars versus blocks		
Follows two-step directions		
Concentrates or attends to self-selected activities for longer periods of time		
Points to and labels objects spontaneously, such as when reading a book		
Coordinates pretend play with other children		
Gains a nominal sense of numbers through counting and labeling objects in a set		
Begins developing concepts about opposites such as big and small, tall and short, in and out		
Begins eveloping concepts about time such as today, tomorrow, and yesterday		

Additional Observations for Cognitive Development

The developmental milestones listed are based on universal patterns of when various traits emerge. Because each child is unique certain traits may develop at an earlier or later age.

SOCIAL DEVELOPMENT		OBSERVED
Birth to Three Months	Date	Comments
Turns head toward a speaking voice		
Recognizes primary caregiver		
Bonds to primary caregiver		
Finds comfort in the human face		
Displays a social smile		
Is quieted by a voice		
Begins to differentiate self from caregiver		
Four to Six Months		
Seeks out adults for play by crying, cooing, or smiling		
Responds with entire body to familiar face by looking at a person, smiling, kicking legs, and waving arms		
Participates actively in interactions with others by vocalizing in response to adult speech		
Smiles at familiar faces and stares solemnly at strangers		
Distinguishes between familiar and nonfamiliar adults and surroundings		
Seven to Nine Months		
Becomes upset when separated from a favorite adult		
Acts deliberately to maintain the presence of a favorite adult by clinging or crying		
Uses adults as a base for exploration, typically		
Looks to others who are exhibiting signs of distress		
Enjoys observing and interacting briefly with other children		
Likes to play and responds to games such as patty-cake and peekaboo		
Engages in solitary play		
Develops preferences for particular people and objects		
Shows distress when in the presence of a stranger		
Ten to Twelve Months		
Shows a decided preference for one or two caregivers		
Plays parallel to other children		
Enjoys playing with siblings		
Begins asserting self		
Begins developing a sense of humor		
Develops a sense of self-identity through the identification of body parts		
Begins distinguishing boys from girls		

The developmental milestones listed are based on universal patterns of when various traits emerge. Because each child is unique certain traits may develop at an earlier or later age.

SOCIAL DEVELOPMENT		OBSERVED
Thirteen to Eighteen Months	Date	Comments
Demands personal attention		
Imitates behaviors of others		
Becoming increasingly aware of the self as a separate being		
Shares affection with people other than primary caregiver		
Shows ownership of possessions		
Begins developing a view of self as autonomous when completing tasks independently		
Nineteen to Twenty-Four Months		
Shows enthusiasm for company of others		
Views the world only from own, egocentric perspective		
Plays contentedly alone or near adults		
Engages in functional play		
Defends possessions		
Recognizes self in photographs or mirrors		
Refers to self with pronouns such as *I* or *me*		
Categorizes people by using salient characteristics such as race or hair color		
Shows less fear of strangers		
Twenty-five to Thirty-Six Months		
Observes others to see how they do things		
Engages primarily in solitary or parallel play		
Sometimes offers toys to other children		
Begins to play cooperatively with other children		
Engages in sociodramatic play		
Wants to do things independently		
Asserts independence by using "no" a lot		
Develops a rudimentary awareness that others have wants or feelings that may be different than their own		
Makes demands of or "bosses" parents, guardians, and caregivers		
Uses physical aggression less and uses words to solve problems		
Engages in gender stereotypical behavior		

Additional Observations for Social Development

The developmental milestones listed are based on universal patterns of when various traits emerge. Because each child is unique certain traits may develop at an earlier or later age.

EMOTIONAL DEVELOPMENT		OBSERVED
Birth to Three Months	**Date**	**Comments**
Feels and expresses three basic emotions: interest, distress, and disgust		
Cries to signal a need		
Quiets in response to being held, typically		
Feels and expresses enjoyment		
Shares a social smile		
Reads and distinguishes adults' facial expressions		
Begins to self-regulate emotional expressions		
Laughs aloud		
Quiets self by using techniques such as sucking a thumb or pacifier		
Four to Six Months		
Expresses delight		
Responds to the emotions of caregivers		
Begins to distinguish familiar from unfamiliar people		
Shows a preference for being held by a familiar person		
Begins to assist with holding a bottle		
Expresses happiness selectively by laughing and smiling more with familiar people		
Seven to Nine Months		
Responds to social events by using the face, gaze, voice, and posture to form coherent emotional patterns		
Expresses fear and anger more often		
Begins to regulate emotions through moving into or out of experiences		
Begins to detect the meaning of others' emotional expressions		
Looks to others for clues on how to react		
Shows fear of strangers		
Ten to Twelve Months		
Continues to exhibit delight, happiness, discomfort, anger, and sadness		
Expresses anger when goals are blocked		
Expresses anger at the source of frustration		
Begins to show compliance to caregivers' requests		
Often objects to having playtime stopped		
Begins eating with a spoon		
Assists in dressing and undressing		
Acts in loving, caring ways toward dolls or stuffed animals, typically		
Feeds self a complete meal when served finger foods		
Claps when successfully completing a task		

The developmental milestones listed are based on universal patterns of when various traits emerge. Because each child is unique certain traits may develop at an earlier or later age.

EMOTIONAL DEVELOPMENT (continued)	OBSERVED	
Thirteen to Eighteen Months	Date	Comments
Exhibits autonomy by frequently saying "no"		
Labels several emotions		
Connects feelings with social behaviors		
Begins to understand complicated patterns of behavior		
Demonstrates the ability to communicate needs		
May say "no" to something they want		
May lose emotional control and have temper tantrums		
Shows self-conscious emotions such as shame, guilt, and shyness		
Becomes frustrated easily		
Nineteen to Twenty-Four Months		
Expresses affection to others spontaneously		
Acts to comfort others in distress		
Shows the emotions of pride and embarrassment		
Uses emotion words spontaneously in conversations or play		
Begins to show sympathy to another child or adult		
Becomes easily hurt by criticism		
Experiences a temper tantrum when goals are blocked, on occasion		
Associates facial expressions with simple emotional labels		
Twenty-Five to Thirty-Six Months		
Experiences increase in number of fears		
Begins to understand the consequences of basic emotions		
Learns skills for coping with strong emotions		
Seeks to communicate more feelings with specific words		
Shows signs of empathy and caring		
Loses control of emotions and throws temper tantrums		
Able to recover from temper tantrums		
Enjoys helping with chores such as cleaning up toys or carrying grocery bags		
Begins to show signs of readiness for toileting		
Desires that routines be carried out exactly as has been done in the past		

Additional Observations for Emotional Development

The developmental milestones listed are based on universal patterns of when various traits emerge. Because each child is unique certain traits may develop at an earlier or later age.

Appendix I
Anecdotal Record

SAMPLE ANECDOTAL RECORD

Child's name: ___Reyshawn___ Date of birth: __5/13_____

Observer's name: ___Chris___ Observation date: __3/31_____

Behavioral description of observation:

During diapering, Reyshawn took the clean diaper and covered his face. He then removed the diaper and began smiling and laughing.

Interpretation of observation:

Reyshawn was initiating a favorite game that we have played during diapering in the past. He is beginning to demonstrate advancements in his language and communication as well as his social skills.

SAMPLE ANECDOTAL RECORD

Child's name: _____ Date of birth:_____

Observer's name: _____ Observation date:_____

Behavioral description of observation:

Interpretation of observation:

Appendix J
Panel Documentation

A panel is a two-dimensional display to communicate with others the learning that occurred during an activity. Panels present the learning of a group of children; thus, different children and their work must be featured. For ease of reading, you should neatly handwrite or type your message. Then, adhere all sections mentioned in the following list on a foam board, poster board, or trifold board.

A panel should contain the following information:

♡ Title of the activity
♡ A record of the children's *actual* words while engaging with the materials or interacting with peers
♡ Artifacts to document representations of the children's thinking—drawings paintings, writings, and/or graphs—or photographs of the children's work on sculptures, creative drama/movements, or roles during dramatic play
♡ A narrative that highlights and explains what learning and interactions occurred

To fulfill the goal of communicating with others, the panel will need to be displayed in a prominent location. Invite others to look at and converse about the children's work. Include the children as part of the audience by reviewing their work as a way to promote language, cognitive, and social development. Also, build on the experience during future activities.

For additional resources on making panels, see:

Gandini, L., & Pope Edwards, C. (Eds.). (2001). *Bambini: The Italian approach to infant/toddler care.* New York: Teachers College Press.

Helm, J. H., Beneke, S., & Steinheimer, K. (1998). *Windows on learning: Documenting young children's work.* New York: Teachers College Press.

Pope Edwards, C., Gandini, L., & Forman, G. (Eds.). (1993). *The hundred languages of children.* Norwood, NJ: Ablex.

Appendix K
Lesson Plan

Name: _____ Date: _____

Developmental area: _____

Child's developmental goals:

Materials:

Preparation:

Nurturing strategies:

Variations:

Infant Daily Communication:
Home to Center

Infant's name: _____ Parent's name: _____

Day/date: _____ Time of arrival: _____ Time of departure: _____

FILLED IN BY PARENT:

Infant seems:	[ ] Normal, typical
	[ ] Bit fussy
	[ ] Not acting like usual
Infant slept:	[ ] Soundly
	[ ] Woke up several times
	[ ] Did not sleep well
Infant ate:	[ ] Meal before coming _____
	[ ] Bottle or nursed before coming
	[ ] Snack before coming
	[ ] Nothing
Infant changed:	[ ] Bowel movement Time _____
	[ ] Wet Time _____

SPECIAL INSTRUCTIONS FOR TODAY:

_____

_____

_____

_____

_____

Parent's signature: _____

Caregiver's signature: _____

Adapted with permission from New Horizon Child Care, Inc.

Infant Daily Communication: Center to Home

Date: _____ Check-in time: _____

Read infant's daily communication: Home to center _____

FILLED IN BY CAREGIVER:

Infant slept: Asleep _____   Awake _____

                Asleep _____   Awake _____

Infant ate: Time _____   What _____   Amount _____

                Time _____   What _____   Amount _____

                Time _____   What _____   Amount _____

Infant changed: Time _____   Wet _____   Bowel movement _____

                Time _____   Wet _____   Bowel movement _____

                Time _____   Wet _____   Bowel movement _____

INTERACTIONS/ACTIVITIES: *(Description of adult interaction, developmental tasks, and activities that sustained child's interest)*

_____

_____

_____

NOTES TO PARENTS:

_____

_____

_____

Caregiver's signature: _____

Parent's signature: _____

We need: [ ] Diapers   [ ] Wipes   [ ] Formula   [ ] Baby food

          [ ] Change of clothing [ ] Blankets [ ] Other: _____

Adapted with permission from New Horizon Child Care, Inc.